The College Handbook They Never Gave You

The Ultimate How-To Guide for Success in College

Dan Stevens

Table of Contents

Introduction

It's the summer before your first semester of college. Only a few more months until you embark upon the journey and adventure that will be the "college experience" that everyone told you about. You have no idea what to expect, but you do know that it is going to be a lot different from the structure of high school. Thankfully, your college has put together an "orientation" meeting for you, which theoretically should shed some light on what is to come in the not too distant future. You are told that you will also get a chance to pick your classes under the guidance of an advisor.

Orientation day arrives. You and maybe 50-200 other students are tightly packed into a room as some school official tries their best to explain away some of the concerns and anxiety you may be facing heading into college, but to little or no avail. They simply tell you what you've already been told, and you still don't know what the heck to expect.

Then suddenly you are thrown in front of a computer. Some advisor states "okay, go to this website and pick your classes." You simply have no idea what classes to pick. You don't even know what your major requires you to take, and yet this person, who by the way is not at all familiar with your specific major, wants you to pick your classes perfectly on a whim. You realize relatively quickly that the order of classes that you take is incredibly important, so what this person is asking you to do is plan virtually your entire college career blindly. So you do as they ask and this propels you headlong into your first days of college. "Orientation" they called it? Right.

You start your first days of college and it all turns

out to very, VERY different from anything you had ever done before. Two tests that make up 60% of your total grade for the class, and difficult homework assigned almost daily, and you have a professor who is not qualified to teach. And this is the case for 4 or 5 classes! You probably are wondering at this point whether or not you will achieve success in these classes, let alone college. And if you are to be successful and make the most of college and your coursework, you are likely wondering how you're going to do it. Wouldn't have been nice if your orientation would have given you a handbook telling you how to manage your classes and how to achieve the level of success you desire, and potentially how to use your education to find a job eventually?

If you have or are currently experiencing something similar to the above, you are certainly not alone! It seems that the consensus for most undergrads is that from Day 1 (orientation) they are in the dark when it comes to succeeding in school even when they are a few semesters into their studies. At best, many (myself included) stumble through their academics for a few semesters and eventually learn "how to college," but still with a great degree of uncertainty. And even if they figure out how to succeed academically, there is practically no help when it comes to landing a job or internship after they graduate.

They say that hindsight is 20/20. That is, looking back, it is easier to see how you could have done things better and how you could have maximized your success or reduced the amount of trial and error. This book is written to provide you with that hindsight in advance.

This book is vastly different from any other book on this or a similar topic, as it provides insights from two different vantage points. It is simultaneously written from the prospective of a student who has recently graduated from a small four-year state school in Pennsylvania, and also from the perspective of a Teacher's Assistant (TA), which has many of the same duties as a professor in terms of teaching. Going from an undergrad student to a 'mini-professor' in the time frame of about two years has given me insight into the mind of both the professor and the student, thus allowing me to see how the two perspectives naturally interact with one another. This jump eventually lead me to think "man, had I known that professors see things this particular way when I was a student, I would have done things much differently!" The aim of this book is highlight and detail hundreds of successful strategies from both perspectives; strategies that I have learned and used myself as a student, and strategies that I learned would take full advantage of the mindset of a professor. These are tried and true strategies that have been used to achieve success for myself, my peers, and many of my students. Check out the table of contents for a brief overview of these strategies!

Additionally, this book not only strives to help you maximize success in your education, it also aims to provide insights into how you can tailor your education perfectly to the job you want after graduation, and how to actually GET that job. The strategies at the tail end of this book are the very ones that I had used to land a well-paying job as a Software Developer within a week of graduating (had the interview on the day of my last final… that was crazy) in addition to being accepted into a PhD program in Mathematics the following fall semester. My peers and a few of my own students have used these and similar strategies to achieve success in the job market as well! They work like magic!

This book is written with the hard-working student in mind. I don't consider myself terribly gifted or smart per say, so I don't attribute much to innate ability as much as I do a solid work ethic. You do not by any means need to be a genius to do well in school, but having tenacity and drive is paramount to achieving success. If you are willing to work hard and are given solid resources that help you work smarter and not harder, you can achieve any degree of success that you like, whether it is in school or life in general. This book provides many tools to aid you on your way to success. So if you supply the drive and work ethic in tandem with the tools provided in this book, college will be simply at your mercy. So let's get started!

Section A: Foundations for Success; The Mindset

Chapter 1: Your "Why"

Why are you going to college? Seriously... Why have you decided to dedicate 2-4 years of your life to this project called "higher-education"? For some, the answer to this question is on the tip of their tongue. They know what they want to do for the rest of their lives and they have their sights set on a very clear and decisive goal. They know what they love to do, and they can see themselves doing it day in and day out for many years to come. For others, they may not know exactly what they want to do just yet but they have been told that college is one way to find out. They know that those who earn a college degree in virtually any field are likely to make more money in their lifetime than someone without that degree. They also may have a feel for what they are good at or what they might be interested in doing as their major, but aside from that, they don't exactly have a clear vision for the future, post-graduation. You yourself may resonate with one of these scenarios. Whether you already know what you want to do or even if you are simply testing the waters for a while, both are perfectly legitimate. The end gain of what you want to get out of your education and the years that come afterward serve as your "why."

On a grander scale your "why" represents a vision you have for your life and why you do what you decide to do every day. It is the reason you put in the hours of study. It is the reason you work ceaselessly at your job every week. Your "why" is what *fuels you* whether or not you are aware of it consciously. It has the power to see you through any obstacle or setback you may encounter. It can motivate you when, externally, nothing else will. Every day you devote time and energy toward meeting some goal. Think about it. What is it that you do every day? Why is it that you do those things? What end does it meet for you? Does it provide you comfort or pleasure? Does it challenge and excite you? Does it push you to somewhere beyond where you currently stand today? Every day this time you devote has a purpose. The great part is you can learn to use this to your advantage! You can learn to determine both the purpose and the actions you take to meet that purpose! So I ask you again: Why do you do what you do on a daily basis? And now for the harder question: Do these things serve you and the goals you have set for yourself?

But what are your goals? Well for one, you probably want to graduate with some form of degree to your name, and you probably want to do this in a reasonable amount of time. If you already have a vision for what you want to do after school your goal is likely crystal clear in your mind. Perhaps your vision is of having a great job that pays well. Perhaps you dream of supporting a family with your future career. Maybe you'd like to start a business someday. You decisively have something you are working toward over the next several years and you are willing to put in the work to get there. If you don't necessarily have an end-goal in mind, but want to try things out to see "what fits" with your interests and expertise, this too can be a goal you can work toward! In either case, you have classes to attend and assignments to complete every day. Each assignment will get you closer either to your dream career, or it will help you decide whether or not this field is for you. Both knowing and not knowing where you want to go gives you something to work toward. On one hand, the end is always in sight regardless of how far away it might actually be and you strive to reach that potential. On the other hand, all effort put forth is designed to help you find your calling and to discover your potential. Both helps you determine the type of person you want to become and both will get you there.

Every day is a new day and every day matters. Every day will either get you to your goal or pull you further away from it if you don't use it wisely. Every action has a purpose. So what is your purpose right now? What are you striving for? What is your “why”?

It isn't necessary that you figure that out right now. You've likely got a long way to go before graduating and your “why” is something that can be learned along the way. But the sooner you know it, the sooner you can tap into the power that comes from having a purpose for every action you take.

It should also be mentioned that your why can

change! As you go through school your experiences will shape you as a person. You will change and grow in ways that you cannot even fathom. If you are at the tail end of your college career you know this to be true. Through your time and hard work, and even as a part of your social life, your values will change. For some this means a dramatic shift, but for others it is a little bit more subtle. Things that were once extremely important to you may fade into something completely trivial, and likewise, things you thought were trivial now hold extreme importance. Along with this comes a shift in perspective. The way you see yourself and the world around you shifts in line with your ever changing beliefs and values. Thus, the reason you do what you do might change in turn. You may even find that you don't value your major as much as you used to and you find another more appealing. This is okay and happens more often than you may think! If your “why” changes, it is only natural and a part of being human. So go with it!

Do what you are passionate about. If you haven't found your passion or purpose just yet, keep searching and allow your life to flow as adaptively as water. Follow your gut. It somehow already knows where you want to go and who you are to become.

Chapter 2: Tried and Failed Mentality

Structuring

You set out on this massive two-to-four-year endeavor. You were successful in high school and now things have changed drastically from the difficulty of classes to the time you now alone are responsible for structuring. As you may be aware at this point, it isn't an easy endeavor to say the least. It's a constant uphill battle every step of the way. And along the way, so many people are going to drop out; be it transferring to a different school, or dropping out of college altogether. At the school I attended, as many as half dropped out in their freshman year! Why? They suddenly found themselves held to a higher standard than what they were accustomed to. They couldn't mature, adapt, and gain the mindset required to be successful. You won't let that happen though. You have a goal in mind. You have something you have taken to heart that is worth working hard for. Everyone is fast off the starting line at the beginning of their education. Few have the tenacity, willpower, and right mindset that will see them through to the end even through the inevitable ups and downs. But you're here to succeed to the highest degree and failure isn't an option for you. So what exactly is that mindset that will see you through to graduation? Moreover, how to do we go about cultivating it?

It's been said that inventor and entrepreneur Thomas Alva Edison attempted 1000 times to create the world's first electricity powered incandescent lamp (read: light bulb). Worded a slightly different way, he *failed* 1000 times before the light bulb lit. When was the last time you tried something more than 10 times before you called it quits? I certainly can't say that I have. But this guy decided that he was going to stick with it until he got the result he wanted. Had he not, we'd all likely still be in the dark and you wouldn't be reading this electronically right now. Edison saw that there is good in failing, because it put him one step closer to his goal with every single attempt. This is precisely the mindset that we need to cultivate in order to be successful; to see it through until you reach the goal you set out and worked so hard to attain.

Recall back to when you were a kid. You were probably taught how to ride a bike at a fairly young age. You may not remember the exact things you were thinking, but you probably remember that you fell down more times than a child can likely count at that age. But since you now know how to ride a bike (assuming you learned of course), you know that you had to fail your way to success. You know that as a kid you did not stop until you were riding that bike perfectly. Kids have this tenacity about them. They don't care that much if they fall or fail. They just get right back up and try again. Especially in the case of riding a bike, very few kids throw in the towel before they are riding. But somehow along the way to adulthood most people learn to not get back up when they fall down. They learn after a handful of attempts that they simply weren't made to succeed in that area. What happened along the way from age 4 or 5 to age 18? I can't claim to know the answer, but the pattern for success is clear. Sometimes it will take 1000 tries before getting it right. Sometimes it will hurt so badly to get back up and just keep going. But nonetheless, in order to achieve success in anything, we must be willing to fail at first. Just like a kid learning how to ride a bike, you keep trying again and again until you get the result you want. And you will stop at nothing until you get there. In all your endeavors in life, become a kid again. Stop caring that you failed and keep pressing forward.

Learn From Your Failures

In addition to trying over and over again to reach your goals, at each attempt you must also be willing to learn from your mistakes. If at each attempt you learn nothing, then you cannot make diligent progress toward your goal. It would be like starting completely fresh with every attempt. Edison and his colleagues didn't simply try every substance known to man as a filament for that light bulb. They learned from each substance, and determined why it didn't work. In turn, they eventually were able to discern what a viable substance for a filament could be. The lesson here is thus: **The more you can learn from each of your failures the more rapidly you will progress toward your goal.** Necessarily, the less you learn, the more slowly you will progress. So at each failed attempt, try to learn as much as you can from the experience before trying again.

Reframing Your Thoughts

It should be mentioned that when you seek to learn from your mistakes that you must maintain a mentality of positivity and confidence. Many people, when they fail may start to beat themselves up and create negativity within the confines of their mind. Self-defeating beliefs such as "I'm no good at this, but I'm trying anyway" or "I was so stupid to do it that way" are commonplace in so many adults. When attempting anything, we tend to be so hard on ourselves. We generate so much negative self-talk that we can render ourselves completely inactive. We stop trying because of this. So while you are working toward your goals adopt a positive mindset that builds you up instead of breaking you down. Replace negative self-talk with more self-loving, kind, and productive thoughts such as "Well, that didn't work as I had hoped... What if I tried it this other way?" or "That worked a lot better than the last time I tried!" Positive self-talk is far and away one of the most useful tools that will help you to be successful at anything you try. The next time you attempt something, such as a homework assignment on a topic you've never seen before, keep tabs on your thoughts. Are they generally negative? Ask yourself at times you catch these negative thoughts how you could replace them with more loving, kind, and productive thoughts. This at first takes a lot of work, but over time your brain will rewire itself to think in this new way on a regular basis. It will eventually be just as natural as riding a bike.

Record Your Progress for Long-Term Endeavors

When working toward your goal when it seems so far away, it is all too easy to become discouraged by your supposed lack of progress. In the absence of evidence that you are indeed moving forward, you may feel that you are never going to reach your target, and you may simply give up. One really useful trick that I have found to be encouraging is to have a way of monitoring your progress; a way to see that, even though it seems like you aren't getting very far on the surface, you actually *have* made a lot of progress. This can take the form of a journal, 'before-and-after' photos, or a log book. You can use anything that allows you record your progress on a regular basis.

The metaphor I use often when discussing this is the example of the person going to the gym to lose weight. If you are doing things right and safely, losing weight via exercise and dieting takes time and a lot of effort. The progress you see is small from day to day or week to week. It is so small that often it is difficult to remember anything different from what you see in the mirror from one day to the next. But if your goal is to lose weight in the gym, if you have a way of making benchmarks, that is, keeping track of your body statistics, you can refer back to these in times where you feel you aren't going anywhere. If you are ever in doubt about your progress, you can just whip out your benchmark logs and review where you were versus where you are today. It is incredibly encouraging to see your progress and that what you are doing is actually working for you! Make a habit of tracking your progress, and review it often!

Examples of benchmarking for school related tasks are not limited to the following:

- Logging the number of hours you spend studying
- Recording the number of homework problems you have done
- Logging the number of pages you have read of your textbooks
- Developing a rating system for ‘how good you

are' at a particular topic in a class

- Creating a weekly to-do list and keeping track of how many tasks you get done each day
- (My Favorite) create little pieces of paper, each with a goal listed on it, and as you complete each goal, tape the piece of paper on the wall. Build a wall from these little "bricks"

Recall Your Why

Like we discussed in the last chapter, the power knowing exactly why you are working so damn hard and why you are willing to fail and try again is immeasurable. In the down moments, when it seems like life is beating you down at every turn as you try so desperately to reach your goal, when it feels like you just don't want to get back up one more time, recall your "why." Remember why exactly you set out to accomplish your goal. What imagery comes to mind when you visualize your goals? What does it feel like? What does it smell like? Think of all the positive things that will come your way once you reach your goal. Then quietly remind yourself that in order to get there, you have to be willing to try just one more time and keep pressing onward.

Getting Excited to Try Again and Keep Working

Every now and then you will have to call it quits for the day until you can start working toward your goal again. Once that happens, it can be really challenging to motivate yourself to want to start the next day, especially if the work you have to do to progress is particularly painful or cumbersome. One of my personal favorite Jedi Mind Tricks that I use on myself is as follows: **psych yourself up when you aren't working**. That is, get excited for the prospect of being able to work toward your goal. This is tightly coupled with the last tip. For example, suppose you have a test coming up and studying is typically a pain. You know you are going to study but you aren't looking forward to it. Instead of focusing on the obligation of studying, focus on the fact that once you start, you will have mastered that much more material, you will be better prepared for your exam, and you have less that you now need to worry about studying in the future! Get excited about the opportunity to work toward your goal rather than seeing it as an obligation. You will have so much more energy when you next decide to attack your goal. As with all things of the mind (which is a creature of habit), the more often you do this, the more automatic it will become.

Conclusion

Whether or not you like the school you are currently attending or whether or not you got into the Ivy League School at the top of your applications list, you are where you are now. You therefore have to make a decision: "Will

I make the most of this situation and the environment I find myself in? Or will I do what I can just to get by, tolerating what has to get done to graduate?" Most people don't make this decision consciously. Either they have been motivated for a good deal of their life and making the most of what they have is inherent in their very being, or they succumb to the stressors and the ups and downs of life, tiptoeing around hoping not to get hurt along the way. And what is unfortunate is that a vast majority of people decide on the latter, whether they realize it or not. They are conditioned by the very fabric of reality that life is going to beat them down time and time again, and getting back up seems near impossible. Life is incredibly hard and cruel more often than not, and it is almost instinctual to cling to the few comforts that exist around us. While this mentality makes sense from an evolutionary standpoint and it certainly feels good in light of the trials and tribulations that stand ahead of you, it is *so poisonous* to all that you wish to achieve and to the person you want to become.

At this age, nearly everyone you will talk to will claim that they want to be successful. They will have high hopes and expectations; a twinkle in their eyes. So full of aspiration and zeal for life, they head out and try to make a name for themselves. But then reality hits hard and fast, and before they know it, they find a deep seated fear that reaching their dreams may not be possible or will certainly not be the easy step-by-step process they had envisioned at the outset of college. When all seems hopeless is precisely when the mentalities mentioned above need to kick in; when a person is down and out and getting up is more difficult than staying down. This is when you shine; when the going gets tough.

So what happens to the person who succumbs to life's down moments? What happens to their dreams and goals? The ideas and dreams they had for their future will seem more distant than they did before. They realize that the journey is going to be tumultuous and they will lose confidence in themselves. They will think that they don't have what it takes. They will lose that motivation and that drive that was once present at the outset and they won't want to endure every single battle that will take place along the way. Their dreams slip away and they will decide to settle. The future veterinarian or medical doctor will lower their expectations so as to lessen their pain and the work involved. They may in this light decide to strive for a veterinary tech position or an outpatient nurse as these paths require less perceived pain (don't get me wrong, these are great and necessary professions). The dreams they once had are dead and gone and if they are lucky, they will not have to endure this cycle again and again. Unfortunately some do experience this several times over, dropping their standard for what they want to achieve every single time. This is exactly what happens when people drop out of college (barring external influences such as lack of funding). They simply give up.

On the other hand, we have the individuals who view the challenges they face as an opportunity; an opportunity to better themselves and strengthen their character and resolve. They get knocked down and they make the conscious decision to get back up again stronger than they ever were before. They find a way out of no way. If they don't have the opportunities or the resources they need, they make them. They keep their eye on what they decided they wanted out of life and out of their education and they go for it day in and day out. If life gets hard they don't quit! They work harder to overcome the obstacles and what they think is impossible. They make the decision consciously or unconsciously at the outset of their education, wherever they find themselves and in whatever their situation, to make the most out of their circumstances. These people are the success stories out of the news and history books. The journey for those who persist is going to be hard, yes. Ultimately however, they find a way to make their dreams into a reality. They build the character and the tenacity required to endure this process, and they become the best versions of themselves along the way. And this is exactly the type of person you already are whether or not you realize it yet.

Chapter 3: Your Environment Matters!

We all start out as a single celled organism; a sperm united with an egg, and nine months later we end up a fully grown infant. How does one cell grow to be such a complex organism? How does our DNA know when and how to produce muscle, skin, and brain cells throughout those nine months? While the answer to that question still lies relatively poorly understood, research suggests that the cell, via its DNA, knows to produce other types of cells, such as muscle or nerve cells, because of the environment in which it finds itself. Different nutrients are present in the womb at different points during those nine months of pregnancy. Different oxygen levels, different molecules, different hormone levels, all of which change as the fetus grows. Throughout the nine months of pregnancy, in theory, we are so heavily influenced by our environment. And once we are born, what changes? Do we not learn most behavior and language from our parents? Do we not learn virtually everything during infancy from our parents and siblings? And taking this a step further, you may be able to see the influence others and your circumstances have had on you, your beliefs, and your life as a whole. Since the moment of conception, we are shaped and molded by our environment whether or not you want to admit it. Learning to understand the variable of environment and the role it plays in your life is so instrumental to your success. More importantly, it is crucial to learn how to manipulate this variable in such a way that you guarantee yourself success. In this chapter, we seek to do just that.

The Aim in Academia

As mentioned in the last few paragraphs, we are naturally and necessarily shaped by all factors in our environments, for better or for worse. So putting yourself in an environment where you can thrive is imperative to your success in academics and life in general. In broad terms, you likely know at this point what your major is or is going to be, and potentially you know what type of job you would like to have after you graduate. You also know that there are dozens if not hundreds studying the same topics as yourself and they may even have similar career aspirations. Naturally as students we will cluster with those who have similar interests as ourselves for both a sense of camaraderie and as a sort of academic springboard, that is, those who may be able to help with particular coursework struggles you may be experiencing. This is your oh-so critical environment at this stage of your life, at least in part. As success-minded students we seek to leverage this small microcosm as a means to achieving our utmost potential.

The Optimal Environment for Success

So what does the best possible environment look like; the one that will help you become the best student, peer, potential new-hire, you can be?

Not Being the Best

While it may seem like a fantastic idea to be the best in your field or the best at what you do, this at times can actually serve as a hindrance to your true potential. Think of it this way: suppose you had a cousin in third grade that just learned how to multiply and divide numbers. You, being a college student, have already mastered this skill. So, if you wanted to improve your own mathematical abilities, you probably wouldn't seek tutoring from your cousin. This is the same in any venue of life. If you want to improve yourself in some particular way, it doesn't do you any good to surround yourself with people you can't learn as much from. Instead seek to surround yourself with people who are, to varying degrees, better than you in a particular area. They can and will aid you in your endeavors and will provide insights that you never could have learned otherwise. While it may seem daunting to be among people who may make you feel inferior, it is certainly and ultimately for the better.

A good rule of thumb to follow is thus: if you are the best in your current peer group, seek to be around others who already are where you want to be. The natural need to feel like you "measure up" can be an incredibly powerful motivator. Just being among those who are great at what they do will give you a boost of energy and zeal to improve. It will also give you a solid dose of humility from time to time, but this too is a very good thing!

Potential for Upward Mobility and Improvement

This idea branches directly off the last. We know

that if we surround ourselves with people who are already where we want to be, we can more easily achieve that level of mastery ourselves via their guidance and simply the nature of being in said environment. But in addition to this, outside the realm of where people are directly involved, it is also incredibly important to put yourself in an environment that gives you the potential to advance in a particular area. Let's suppose that you are trying to determine whether to major in Computer Engineering or Computer Science. Let us also suppose that you don't really care as much one way or the other. You have been told that the Computer Engineering program is easier than Computer Science. Furthermore you are told that the Computer Science program offers graduate level classes whereas the Engineering program does not. You know that you only want to get a Bachelor's Degree at this point, so it seems that the easier Computer Engineering program may be the way to go. But you also know that working through the computer science program and taking those grad classes would greatly improve your skillset AND make you more marketable when you apply for a job. Hence you decide to put yourself in the environment that promotes upward mobility, i.e. grad classes, and self-improvement.

Whenever possible, seek out the environment that has the greatest potential for you to improve yourself and your skillset even if it seems like it would be incredibly challenging compared to the alternative. It's like being a freedom-bound goldfish in a tiny fishbowl versus an aquarium. There is always much more you can do for yourself if you are in a "bigger" environment, so to speak.

Environments that Challenge You

There is an old analogy that works well for this idea. When you go to the gym to lift and you want to strengthen and train your muscles, the only way they will grow is if you put stress on them and challenge them. Only then will they adapt. Similarly, if you don't exercise your muscles at all, what happens? The muscle atrophies and dies (not literally… usually.) Likewise, with anything you seek to do or achieve, in order to grow you must seek to challenge yourself. Otherwise, you may run the risk moving backwards in your progress.

For example, suppose you are majoring in Psychology. You approach your third and fourth year and you still need to have five electives in Psychology in order to graduate. However, your program allows you to take either upper-level undergraduate courses to satisfy this requirement or to take graduate level courses instead. While you know that the undergrad electives will be easier than their grad-level counterparts, you also know that you have a lot more to gain in terms of expertise by taking the grad-level variant. This is exactly what it would mean to put yourself in an environment that challenges you. You directly seek out situations where you are challenged and forced to adapt and succeed. That which you gain by doing so vastly dwarfs the skills and expertise you would acquire without challenging yourself and your abilities. The only way you grow in life is through facing adversity and overcoming it.

Access to a Bounty of Resources

Not only is it of critical importance to put yourself in an environment in which you can improve and learn from others, it is also crucial to be in a place where you have many resources at your disposal. These can take the form of faculty, peers (especially upperclassmen), mentors, useable labs and equipment, career resources, or any host of things that may be able to help you reach your goals. While it may not seem clear at the moment where you could use these resources, the act of simply familiarizing yourself to what is available can and will help you when you need them.

One way to determine if a set of resources will be of value to you is by assessing what exactly you are trying to achieve. This could be in the form of a career choice, a very accurate description of the job you'd like to have, or maybe just a loose idea of something you'd like to do either while in school or once you graduate. The more you know about yourself in this way, they more ably you will determine what you need to get you to your goal. This is even true if you don't know where you want to go just yet! There are resources for that too! Simply put, determine where you are going, and what you are lacking to get there. At that point, resource value can easily be determined.

First and foremost, familiarize yourself with your own department. Determine as early as possible the resources they have available to you and others in your program. They may be able to assist future grads in their hunt for a job, or provide tools necessary to determine a solid career path. Usually your department will be able to assist you in many ways, and some of them may surprise you. So be sure to take the time and get to know what is offered right on your doorstep before strolling out.

Investigate what your school as a whole offers by way of resources as well. They may host several clubs or organizations that you can be a part of that also align with your interests or career choice. If you seek these out and involve yourself, you open yourself up to even more resources, ideas, and connections with people who can help you.

Overall, the aim is to put "feelers" out to determine what you have at your disposal in terms of resources. Be aware of "meta"-resources, which, like mentioned above, are resources that may lead to other resources simply by being in a particular environment or with a particular group of people. Resourcefulness is easily the most important skill you can acquire. This is an awesome way to cultivate this skill and also help you reach your goals.

Leadership and Teaching Opportunities

Unsurprisingly, one of the things that employers seek in potential new-hires is the capacity to lead. Why, you may ask? Because leadership demonstrates a sense of initiative and drive in a particular individual. The employer knows that they will not need to "hold their hand" for very long and that this new-hire will take charge of their new position the moment they are able and do the best work that they can muster with a sense of pride. A leader is one who wants to be successful and will work for it. Employers know this, and surely, they will always bet on the interviewee who demonstrates critical leadership qualities. It is easier to bet when you already know who the winners are.

On your campus, there are a plethora of different activities in which you can serve the role of a leader. It could be as simple as leading a team project, or tutoring in your campus's learning center. As long as you are the one primarily calling the shots in some regard and people listen to you for instruction or for information, that is the type of environment which will serve you best. And if you cannot find a way to serve as a leader, you can always make up a role. That is, you can start your own group project, team, or organization. You get extra leadership bonus points if you take this kind of initiative!

Section B: How to Do Well In Your Coursework

In this section, we will be discussing many tactics that can be employed to make the most of your time and how to work efficiently for all of your classes. Far and away, if you employ just a few of these tips, you will find yourself doing incredibly productive work, learning at a faster and better rate than most of your peers. We will cover how to make the most of the learning resources you have available to you, and how to "work the system" in a way. That is, we will be taking advantage of the psychology of professors, testing environments, and study regimes to fully enhance your education. We will also discuss the advantages of building up little habits which, if you do them consistently, will have a HUGE impact on your success. So let's get started!

Chapter 4: Time Scheduling and the Student Workload

What Most Students Are Up Against

Students in any college-like situation often have a lot on their plate. On average they hold about 4-6 classes per semester and need to keep up with all the work involved in those classes. They often work part-time jobs or internships and participate in a whole host of extracurricular activities. Not to mention they have to make time for friends, exercising, leisure, and sometimes sleep. It's certainly not exactly something that is easy to schedule because from day to day, their schedule will vary wildly. Even from week to week it is challenging because you are constantly being assigned new work to do with varying difficulty. Like juggling 23 balls at once, it can be tricky to keep them all in the air at the same time. This is far and away the most difficult aspect of managing college: staying in control of one's schedule. Well at least it certainly was for me.

Scheduling for most of undergrad for me was an absolute nightmare. In any given semester, I was enrolled in 6-7 classes on average. I also needed to work two part-time jobs to ensure that I had 32-40 hours of work per week because tuition wasn't cheap. I had to throw exercise in there somewhere as well. Sleep? ...I heard about that once. I lived by the seat of my pants, at the mercy of my classes and what life threw at me. Try as I did to stay productive, the entropic hell that was my life quickly saw to it that I burned out. It didn't take long before I was running on empty. I didn't discover the magic that was having a concrete and deliberate schedule until late in my 3rd year. Ever since I made that discovery, I have sworn by it. I have increased my productivity by a factor of three and I suddenly have much more free time than I thought could possibly exist even with such a loaded calendar. So in this chapter we will be building a schedule that is tailor-made to suit your life and your circumstances, aiming to help you to the same degree it helped me. It will be custom-made to consolidate your time and make you as efficient as possible.

One thing should be mentioned at the outset of this however. Because your class schedule changes on a per-semester basis, and likewise your job hours (if you have one) will also change from time to time, you may need to go through this brief procedure repeatedly. There is no "blanket schedule" that will work rain or shine, especially for students. So remember that adaptability and flexibility in your scheduling is crucial.

Scheduling Tools

I recommend for this process using some sort of scheduling app that "blocks off" time hour by hour. Google Calendar is fantastic for this as it gives you a way to visualize your time commitments with literal boxes that fill in time slots. It's even better if you have an app on your phone that does this. Apple i-Devices have the native calendar app. Android also has a scheduling app that should accomplish this as well. If all else fails, you can do this with a spreadsheet.

Scaffolding Your Schedule

Here we will be building up the basic framework for your schedule. These are the inflexible things that can't really be changed such as your class meeting times, your work schedule (which may be more or less flexible in your case), extracurriculars, etc. Anything that has a set time that is beyond your control is what we will be plotting right now. So crack open your app/spreadsheet and enter in all your pre-committed time obligations.

Later we will discuss different methodologies for picking class times that both suit your lifestyle and encourage a strong work ethic (See: "Don't take an 8am class!")

Outside-of-Class Time

Now that we have scheduled the all the inflexible aspects of our week, we will now focus on assigning time for school-related work around the scaffolding we just developed. First we will go into how to schedule this time, then we shall go into why.

The Golden Rule for Study Time

There are many mathematical formulas out there that tell you exactly how many hours per week to spend studying given how many credits you are taking. Numbers such as 2-3 hours for every hour you are in class are often cited as a general rule to follow. So by that logic, with the average of 15 credits per semester (or 15 class hours per week), this puts the average student at 45-60 hours of total school work per week. If taken to the extreme such as my sickening schedule of 21 credits per semester, that puts me at 63-84 hours of work a week on top of my usual 32-40 hours spent at my jobs. 95-124 hours per week total. Note that there are 168 hours per week including weekends. There is no way on God's green earth that I put in that many hours! And there is no way the average student that graduates with good grades puts in 60 hours either! All this to say, the ideal mentioned above is basically non-applicable and nearly useless to most students.

So what's the Golden Rule? What is a reasonable max amount of time to spend on school per day? Based on students I have talked with personally and end of semester polls taken in the classes I have taught, the best scoring students budget 7-9 hours for their school work per day. Incredibly few students budget more than 10 hours per day. Hence, the **Golden Rule: If you are enrolled in 12-18 hours of classes per week, budget 7 to 9 hours a day.** This is all inclusive! That is, this includes the time you spend in class AND the time you spend studying/devoting to homework. What this amounts to is a grand total of 35-45 hours per week. Hey, that looks an awful lot like a full-time job! Seems a little more reasonable, right?

I really don't expect anyone reading this to diligently put in 7 to 9 hours in a day every single day. I sure as hell didn't! Given the chaotic nature of most of our lives in college, it is simply impossible to expect. Moreover, the workload of each student varies significantly. On some days or weeks you will have next to no work to do. On others, you will have a lot more on your plate. So the Golden Rule, as it is put, is a *budget.* Like with finances, some months you go over, some months you save a little. So by *allocating* 6-9 hours a day for school, we are setting a reasonable upper bound. More often than not, you will spend far fewer hours on school if you use your time well (See: Using Study Time Effectively).

You may be asking "Why set a time budget if we aren't going to fully use the time we allocate?" This is a good question with a practical answer. Allocating time for school-related work essentially determines what parts of your day you will devote strictly to studies, and what parts of the day you don't have even *think* about school! That is, once you have everything done that you wanted to accomplish, you are DONE for the day. That's it. No more school. Just play time. If you finish early, fantastic! You are done! If you have a lot to do in a given day and you need to use all 7-9 hours, you are allowed to be done for the day the second you hit your budget! This of course is assuming you aren't facing a deadline tomorrow and you can continue to work into the next day. Thus, there may be times where you go over budget for a few days because of a deadline. That will surely happen. But if you spread your work evenly throughout the week, this surprisingly won't happen very often at all! We will go more in depth with how to use this time efficiently later.

How to Schedule Via the Golden Rule

The idea of using the Golden Rule outlined above was to "chunk" your day into two parts, one where you are working, and one where you are not even thinking about school. So it wouldn't really make much sense to fire your hours out of a shotgun and see what it hits. That is, scattering your hours around each day so you are seemingly almost always working. Then again, some people work better this way. But for most, it will be hard to start again once you have stopped working. This of course is entirely up to you and how you want to work your budget around your courses and other obligations. I personally prefer to keep all my study/homework hours closer to my classes and keep them constrained to the weekdays, Monday through Friday. This allows me to have weekends off. Weekends can also serve as a safety net just in case all hell breaks loose where I need that spare time. But on the whole, I keep my out-of-class work hours tightly clustered with my classes so I can have a concrete "quitting time."

Additionally, I tend to start every day at the same time as my earliest class. For example, if on a Monday, I have an 8am class but on Tuesday or Thursday my earliest class is at 11am, I make sure I still am awake to be on campus and working by 8 am. Doing this gives me consistency and a routine that I don't have to think about. My "quitting time" is the same every day. It also allows me to sleep consistently (which is more important than the amount you get), even if I was out late the night prior (See: Sleep). While beneficial if it can be achieved, this ideal is quite lofty for some. I certainly encourage it because I've seen a good deal of success (and more importantly, happiness) from those who schedule this way, but **it is okay if you want to start certain days a little later,** like if you have an 8am on Monday, but a 10am on Tuesday. Try to keep your start times close though! I can say from much personal experience that it is SO EASY to let your work ethic slip away into the abyss if your start times are too far apart. If you are a night-hawk and prefer to wake up around noon, picking an 8am class is probably something you don't want to do (See: Course Scheduling Hacks).

Now that we have the biggest aspects of our schedule planned out and solidified, the rest of your time is all yours! If you want to be more specific with your school-work time and divide it up by subject, this can also be fruitful (See: Start Your Week Right).

Chapter 5: Using Study/Work Time Effectively

Nearly every student attending college devotes a significant portion of each day or each week to studying and completing assignments. It's only natural and part of the game right? But what significantly varies is the amount of time each person spends on such work. One student may be able to get all their work done in a few hours whereas another student it might take several days. Often it is speculated that the student who gets their work done more quickly is simply better at that subject or they are simply smarter. But this doesn't always have to be the case. While some are naturally more gifted or skilled, others may simply be efficient and effective in the way they work. In this chapter, we will be discussing several ways that you can use your study/work time effectively, thereby reducing the amount of time you spend working and increasing your level of understanding.

Start Your Week Right

There is simply no describing the amount of power you can have over your schedule and also your life if you have already in mind how the week should play out. That is, just the act of knowing what it is you have to get done and by when, your subconscious mind will find a way to get you there. By deliberately scheduling out your assignments and study time prior to starting your week, you will feel more in-control of your time and your willpower. Why? Because the very act of thinking about the things you need to do will help your brain accept as reality those tasks when they need to get done (read: will lead to less procrastination).

At the outset of every week, list all the assignments

you have on your to-do list. Prioritize each assignment according to their due date. That is, write them in order by which ones are due from earliest to latest. Additionally, list all the readings or studying you have to do as well. Determine up front how much time you want to devote to studying and working on each assignment over the course of the whole week. Your first priority should always be to complete first the assignment that is due the earliest. So put each of these assignments into your "study/homework time" schedule blocks according to their due date, with the earliest due assignment listed first. Some people prefer to frontload their work at the beginning of the week so they get it done sooner and can stop worrying about it. Others prefer to spread out their work so they don't feel overwhelmed. Whichever style you prefer, allocate your assignments and work time throughout your pre-scheduled "Study Time" hours (See last chapter if you haven't already). Just make sure you have given yourself enough time to complete your assignments and studies. Also, make sure you deliberately include study time!

Lastly, commit to this schedule, but know also that it can change. It may take you longer or shorter than expected to complete an assignment. If this happens, adjust your schedule accordingly. This by no means is a perfect rigid schedule that will work every time for every week. The student workload varies so much that it is impossible to create a schedule that works perfectly for every student 100% of the time. But it is possible however to make an *adaptable* schedule that works for you. Even if your schedule has to change often, just having one in place gives you a sense of direction. It also gives you a sense of fulfillment when you stick to your commitments!

Use a Timer That Counts Up

While studying or working on virtually any task, I

have found that it helps my focus tremendously to keep a timer running in the background. There is something about having a timer constantly ticking that reminds you to stay focused when your mind wanders. It's a bit of a Jedi mind trick but it works extraordinarily well! Not only does it help focus, but it also makes you want to work faster and get your tasks done sooner. You could even turn this into a game if you want. Make a guess about how long it will take you to finish something and see if you can beat your guess!

Avoid Multitasking

Many students when they work on their assignments or are studying will either have their phone or a computer close by. Nine times out of ten, those devices aren't being used to help with your work and they only serve to distract you. If you have a distraction at the ready while you are working, I guarantee you it will take five times as long to finish your work. And it's not just distractions per say that can slow you down. This is even true if you are trying to work on multiple things simultaneously. If your attention is divided, it takes your brain a good deal of time to switch from one task to another. This is because when you switch from one task to another, your brain has to refocus as if you were starting each task from scratch. Not only that, this constant refocusing makes it more difficult to retain and process information effectively. And if you are doing this many times over the course of a few hours, it can *really* slow you down. So as you sit down and get to work, devote all of your attention to one and only one task. Close all access to easy distractions. Doing this alone can save you time and enhance your studying more than you ever thought possible.

Take Small Breaks to Increase Efficiency

It's kind of a shame, but research has shown that

people cannot focus intensely for more than 40 minutes at any given time. After that the brain is far less productive than inside that 40 minute window. Humans learn best in small spurts. Think of it this way: when was the last time a friend told you something that you needed to remember? Did you have to study it and review it over and over again? Or did your brain just store it once and for all? Most likely, the latter will be the case. Thus, the effect of sporadic learning can actually have more of an impact on overall memory retention; more than we think when compared to the purported efficiency of hours of study without a break.

The rule I and many others use is to work for 30 to 45 minutes straight without distraction. No phone checking; no computer; nothing but you and your work. Then once those 30-45 minutes are up, I allow myself to take a 10-15 minute break. Much to my surprise, this has actually helped with motivation to keep working and has vastly helped with my learning. Odds are it will for you too!

When Possible, Spread Out an Assignment

This goes hand in hand with the above tip, but also to a larger degree. You know when you are working on homework problems or perhaps a large project or paper and you just can't make progress? Sort of like you have writers block or you just can't force your brain to produce ideas? There is a relatively simple solution to this that uses the power of your subconscious mind, and it works marvelously. Take a break from the task! That is, put it off until tomorrow or some other point in time. Your subconscious is a wonderful device that processes information even though you aren't thinking about it. Your brain forms new connections about the subject you are working on even while you are working on something completely unrelated! So by taking a break that spans a few days, you are giving your subconscious the time to process and form these connections. What's the benefit of this you may ask? The moment you start working again, you may be surprised that you can think more effectively and creatively about your assignment, which in turn leads to more effective work. Why? Because your subconscious processing made you better at it while you worked on other things.

Review and Re-review Often

The more time your brain gets to work on a task or on a given topic, the better it gets at it. So combined with the above strategy, by frequently reviewing material you already know every now and then, it becomes really hard to forget material you learned. Psychological research indicates that the first time you learn something, you tend to forget it fairly quickly, but every time you review it, the time it takes to forget it is lengthened. That is, every time you review, the more permanent the information becomes in your mind.

Note that you don't need to review intensely. Like what was mentioned in the last tip, if you spread out your study, you can use the power of your subconscious mind to do a lot of the reviewing for you. So take 5 to 10 minutes every so often to revisit old material even if you already know it. This simple tip will surprise you with how much you are able to remember when you need it most (such as on a test).

Learn to "Skim" Effectively and Use Iterative Learning

We are all taught while in elementary school or perhaps middle school that "skimming", that is reading text quickly, skipping unimportant material, and looking for the key ideas, is an effective and quick way to get the 'gist' of the text. Moreover, using this approach can take less than 1/10 of the time it would take you to read the text normally. However, many people abandon this strategy because it doesn't produce the depth of understanding and comprehension that students often need. Additionally, in order to extract a good deal of information while skimming, you have to be insanely focused. If your mind wanders as it often will while reading, you won't get as much out of your skimming. But even though skimming in the traditional sense is usually not too fruitful, we can adapt the strategy to enhance your efficiency in reading.

While skimming the material, take notes. Write down the key ideas as you find them. Usually these ideas if found in a textbook will be in boldface writing. If you are reading your notes, you probably have a good idea of what the key ideas are as the professor probably made a point to emphasize them. Regardless of what you are skimming, make a point to write and rewire key ideas. This will help you focus much more effectively and more importantly, it will solidify the ideas in your mind and help you memorize them incredibly well.

Another useful tactic to use for reading notes and textbooks is to skim iteratively. That is, make a point to skim and re-skim the material. By doing this, your brain will subconsciously pick up on details you missed the first time you skimmed your text. You will learn more with each time you skim. And since skimming is usually done in a mere fraction of the time it normally takes to read the text, you can get a lot of information from skimming and re-skimming a few times and still save yourself a lot of time!

Reading Textbooks Optimally

Often within textbooks information will be divided

up into sections that span maybe half of a page or slightly more. This is fantastic because it groups ideas nicely together and highlights the most important ones. It also provides an excellent mechanism by which you can study and learn. Every time you finish one of these sections make a point to write down in your notes a short summary of what that section said *in your own words.* This forces your brain to think about work with the information directly using your own vocabulary. This leads to better retention of the facts you have just read. In general, the more ways you interact with information the more you will remember. So by writing things down in your own words, or saying them aloud as you write them, you are forming more connections in your brain as you work through the text -- more connections than if you simply read the material and never did anything with it.

The Value of a Work-Conducive Area

It is underrated how important it is to be in a solid work-conducive environment. That is, one that is free of noise and distractions and potential unrelated conversations. Many students will seek out these bad study places *because* it is an easy distraction. For the sake of your work, DON'T DO THIS! Find a quiet place like the school library in which you can study preferably alone or with one other person (See: Get an Accountability Buddy).

Brief Conclusion

The above is a simple set of strategies that can lead to more productive work and study time. There are a few others that could be placed in this chapter, but have been relegated to the chapter on Procrastination, so check those out as well! As always, change things up to suit yourself and how you work best.

Chapter 6: Making the Most of Class Time

In this chapter we will outline a few strategies on how to make the most out of class time. After all, you are paying thousands for someone to stand up in front of the class and preach at you for hours. Might as well try to get something for your money right?

Strategy 1: Go to Class!

This should almost go without saying, but there are far too many students who cut class regularly for a variety of reasons. Even if the professor sucks at teaching (most aren't trained in teaching, believe it or not) and the material isn't something you find terribly interesting, or worse, the combination of the two, there is still something you can get out of that lecture time. You may learn something that makes you think differently about a particular matter, even if it doesn't pertain to the class itself. I can't tell you how many times I had interesting Computer Science research ideas pop into my head when I was in a dreadful Social Psychology or Differential Equations lecture! Think of it this way: the person standing in front of you is giving you new information in order to augment your understanding in some way. Just by being in that environment, you are exposing yourself to new ideas and new perspectives. Who know, maybe these ideas will help you solve a problem completely unrelated to the class someday! Thus, there is always something to be gained by going to lecture; even if you just sit there mildly focused.

Granted, you may find times where you need to be doing something more valuable than what is being taught in lecture on a given day. You are an adult who can make those decisions and not a soul is going to try to stop you. But just keep in mind when you think about cutting class:

you are paying for that class regardless, and the professor always has something to tell you that is probably worth knowing. If they didn't think they could add to your life in some way via their teaching, they wouldn't be at the lectern.

Strategy 2: Take Notes

That is, unless you have an eidetic memory and can remember verbatim what the professor says. Professors usually teach from a textbook and clutch it pretty tightly. Lectures are often a distillation of what the professor themselves have read from the textbook, and will emphasize key points that the professor feels are important (read: "will be on the test"). So by taking notes, you are doing a couple things. One of which is you are generating a useful review guide that you will need before your next exam. The other is that you are generating something to study later; something that will quickly help you learn and relearn important material. Also, if you reference your notes while you read the textbook, the text material will sink in much more rapidly as you will have a knowledge base already built up for yourself already. That is, it is far easier to relate new material to something you already know than to learn something completely new altogether. Even if you don't ever look at your notes again after class, the very nature of writing something down while in class allows some of that information to stick in your memory. It is the simple action of interacting with the material that can lead to far more efficient learning.

Taking notes will aid you in improving your work and study habits on the whole. It will also help you to remember important information from class itself. And remember: Just because you understood the lecture doesn't mean you're going to remember it perfectly when you go to do your homework or go to study. Thus, note-taking is a good habit to start if you haven't already, and it is a fantastic way to enhance your learning to a much higher level. And also be sure to:

Strategy 3: (15 Tips for) Taking Fantastic Notes

This tip is worth emphasizing on its own. If you already use your notes as study material, then you likely already know the benefits of well-kept notes. But if you don't ever even look at your notes again, the following sub-strategies may help a bit. Students who don't read their notes later often feel like the material they wrote down isn't substantial or well organized enough to use again. While you certainly don't have to write textbook-quality notes every lecture, simply adding a little more structure to your notes can of benefit and prompt you to read your notes later when you are studying. Here are a few note-taking tips that have helped my peers, myself, and many of my students:

Tip 1: Have a separate notebook for each class

Tip 2: Use lined paper to increase natural flow of your notes

Tip 3: Start each lecture on a new page. Put the date at the top. This helps when you review.

Tip 4: Start each new topic covered in class with a new heading/paragraph

Tip 5: Don't just write what the prof writes. Write also the key things they *say*

Tip 6: Add your own thoughts or write in your own words to help with absorption,

Tip 7: But copy down formulas, definitions and facts exactly.

Tip 8: If the professor repeats something, make sure you write it and add some emphasis mark to it

Tip 9: Use phrases and never full sentences. Come up with a shorthand way of writing certain things

Tip 10: Leave space between topics in your notes. You

can fill those in while reading and reviewing.

Tip 11: Fill in details to pertinent material when the professor gets sidetracked.

Tip 12: Don't write every detail mentioned. Stick to key points and fill in details later.

Tip 13: Say your notes to yourself as you write them to help with absorbing the material

Tip 14: Review your notes *while still in lecture* when there's a free moment.

Tip 15: Ask questions if something isn't clear before you write it down.

Strategy 4: Sit in the First or Second Row

Doing this, believe it or not, will prompt you to be more focused, alert and attentive to what is being taught. It's a subconscious sort of thing at work here. Because you are now closer to the professor, who can see into the very souls of only the first two rows, you feel naturally compelled to be more active in lecture. In reality, the professor doesn't expect the front-row students to perform more in class. They just do by nature of their environment. It's only due to the subconscious effect of feeling "watched" more, when in actuality the professor doesn't really care. This is very much an example of putting yourself in the environment of success as we discussed in (Section A). And as such, the success portion usually comes automatically.

Strategy 5: Ask Questions and for Material Clarification

Often students are a bit intimidated to ask questions in class in fear of looking stupid or voicing their ignorance to the entire class. They may also feel like they are holding the class back or wasting class time if they asked for clarification. This is very understandable! Nearly everyone feels this way at some point and its a legitimate concern.

But as it turns out, professors don't really judge as much as it seems and your peers are likely just as lost as you feel, if not more so. Also, professors *want* to hear your questions because *they care* if their students understand what they are saying. Don't get me wrong, there are professors that will be condescending and rude to their students. If this happens to you, it's best not to take it personally. Often, this is a reflection of how the professor feels about their own ability to teach you! So if the professor encourages questions, try your best to ask a few! If speaking in class is still intimidating for you, you can always talk to the professor after class. Remember that they want to help and they do care about their students.

Overcoming the Fear of Speaking in Class

For most of college, I was utterly terrified of speaking up in class. I would sit there quietly in my confusion scribbling away whatever the professor wrote, falling further and further behind with every word that came from the lectern. I had many questions I wanted to ask, but I couldn't bring myself to ask them. It took having a professor that actively teased me for me to open up a little more. I still wasn't asking questions at that point. But this professor was really good at reading body language and would call me out. "You look confused..." he would say as he stared at me, smirking from behind his glasses. I learned quickly that I needed to start asking questions before they were yanked out of me. Though I didn't know I was doing this consciously at the time, I followed the process below to get myself to speak up in class.

1) Make a goal to ask one or two questions per class; questions you know the answer to already
2) After a few weeks, replace one question with one you don't know the answer to
3) After a few more weeks, try to ask two questions

you don't know already

4) At this point, you should feel relatively more comfortable asking most questions, so

5) (optional) test yourself by asking a question you KNOW is stupid

6) If you can do Tip 5 and not break a sweat, you now can ask anything in the world

In retrospect, this process definitely helped me to have more confidence in class. It takes a little to get out of your comfort zone initially, but once you do you will very quickly build up your self-confidence in class and strengthen your character a bit as well.

Strategy 6: Put Your Phone Away and Eliminate Distractions

After all, you're paying your school thousands of dollars for the person behind the podium to teach you something. Your lecturer also can clearly see who is paying attention and who isn't, so be careful they aren't vindictive or passive aggressive... or actively aggressive. I've known professors who have thrown erasers and chalk at students who are blatantly using their phone during lecture. Beware. They do exist. And they have tenure.

Strategy 7: Participate in Lecture/Class Discussions

Some classes will require you to participate in the class discussion beyond simply taking notes and asking questions. If this is the case, being active in the class is one of the best possible ways to learn something. You will be actively engaging the material and using it on the fly. Even if you don't feel confident in the discussion topic, see if there is even a small tidbit you can add here or there. Even if it's a simple "I agree!" it shows the professor that you are trying (and trust me it means a lot!). And even if you are looking for a place where you can say "I agree!" you are still actively engaging the material!

There are also instances where a typical "listen and take notes" style class can become more of a discussion. For instance, in the math classes I run, I ask my students to treat it as a conversation. I ask them to help develop the ideas by prompting and guiding them through the material. They essentially will feel like they invented the formulas and theorems themselves. I've known other TA's and professors who do things similarly as well. So if you find yourself in this sort of situation try to get engaged in the discussion as much as you possibly can. Why? Because the more you are actively involved in the class, the more you will retain. If you are the type to feel self-conscious about speaking up in class, see the latter half of Strategy 5.

Strategy 8: Try to Beat the Prof While Doing Problems

This is simply another tip to fully engage yourself in lectures. This often can be hard to accomplish, but if you are in a math or science class where the professor is working problems on the board, it is pretty easy to try to work ahead in your notes as the professor usually works slowly. This is a great way to get practice doing these problems AND get immediate feedback on your work! Whether or not you actually work it out correctly is not the point really. It's only a bonus if you do. The point is that you are actively engaging your mind in the material. I can promise that more success will come your way if you make a habit of doing this.

Strategy 9: Relating Material to What You Know on the Fly

Learning, by and large, isn't just memorizing, or "figuring things out." In order to fully internalize information so that you never forget it, your brain must create a relationship between what you already know and what you need to know. Sure you could just memorize facts word-for-word, but in order to use those ideas and think about them effectively, you have to create this relationship in your mind. While you are in lecture is a great time to do just that. How? Actively think about how the material you are learning is related to things you have learned previously. In science or math classes, information is very quickly built on top of itself, so you may have to relate old material to the new material. For example, if you want to learn about electrons orbiting the nucleus of an atom, you can relate that to how planets orbit the sun. In other types of classes, like psychology or history (or anything to do with people really) it is easier to relate the material being taught to something that has happened in your life or something that you find interesting. Perhaps you are learning in psychology about Catatonic Schizophrenia and you imagine the last time you sat for hours daydreaming (perhaps even in this class). While the parallel isn't going to match perfectly to what you are learning, it still relates new information to old information in your mind and will allow you to retain it and recall it more easily.

Chapter 7: Downtime, Leisure, and Possibly a Social Life

We previously have developed a schedule that divides your day into two distinct parts: one part for school related tasks, and the other for whatever you want to do. The idea behind doing this, as mentioned before, was to give you a part of the day you can always look forward to; a part of the day where you can cultivate hobbies and potentially a social life (A concept quite foreign to those who tend to work around the clock). And as such, this part of your day is just as crucial as the time you spend working on school related tasks. It allows you to recharge your willpower and enjoy life more.

Socialize Your Way to Success

To be completely honest, I only realized this

recently. When I was in college, I had a part time job that allowed for socializing with my co-workers during slow hours. Outside of that and intermittently talking to my peers while in school, I had a very minimal social life. Then I got to grad school where I didn't have to work a part time job, and interactions with other students are even fewer than that in undergrad. Very quickly I realized that something wasn't right in my life, but I for the life of me I couldn't figure out what was wrong. I mean, I had no deliberate social life in undergrad; I didn't have time for one. And not having one now should be no different, right? Dead wrong. While in undergrad, I actually did have a social life despite what I thought. My social life came from where I worked! I spent 5-8 hours a day talking with people when I was on the clock. Now, in grad school, a social life doesn't come as automatically for me, but after looking into it psychologically, I learned that having a deliberate social life is super important for one's wellbeing.

Despite what many introverts may think, it is a fundamental need of humans to be actively engaged with one another. We are biologically wired to be with others, and when we neglect this need, other parts of our life (such as academics and our relationship with ourselves) tend to suffer. Naturally when things start to go wrong in our lives, we tend to look at what relates to the problem in order to find a solution, neglecting any general internal conflict that may be present. Sometimes the real issue has nothing to do with the trouble you are facing, say academically or in your relationships. When this happens, you may have to look at your life as a whole and figure out where you are 'off-balance.' For hard working college students, it is all too easy to neglect this aspect of what it means to live a balanced life. Thus, make a point to spend time with friends and/or family once you are done with school for the day. The benefits of doing so are endless. Improved physical health, mental health, and overall sense of well-being are just a few. Believe it or not, your grades will improve as well!

Having Hobbies for Balance

While in school, it may seem at times that you do little more than school work, study, and socialize from time to time. By your second year it may feel like you are simply a machine that turns coffee into grades. Your morale and overall satisfaction with your life will certainly wane from time to time. Thus is it important that you break that pattern as soon as you can by incorporating hobbies and other enjoyable tasks into your schedule. Having a solid set of hobbies can benefit you in many ways. They break the work-sleep-work-sleep pattern and help you feel productive in doing something you enjoy for its own sake alone. Hobbies and extracurricular activities challenge you in new ways, beyond the scope of your studies, and give you a wider breadth of skills. They can help to burn off steam and the inevitable stress that accompanies college student life. Not to mention they also give you a way to socialize, depending on the hobby of course. So do your best to find something that you truly enjoy outside of your work; something that gives you a sense of fulfillment. Doing this will have an incredible positive impact on your psychology and your sense of wellbeing.

Sit and Do Nothing (Seriously)

While it is certainly of value to have hobbies and a social life, participating in such activities believe it or not can still sap at your willpower. Not to mention, even while you are busy doing things you enjoy after working for the better part of the day, you will feel that free time fly by. Quickly then you will be at the precipice of the next day, wondering where today went! You may feel like you hadn't the chance to recharge at all. And now you have to attack tomorrow just as hard!

So what is the solution to this dilemma? How can you still have hobbies and a social life and feel like you have had adequate "recharge time"? At the end of the day, before you decide to go to bed, just sit by yourself somewhere comfortable and do nothing. That's right. Stop all activity and work, turn off your phone's notification system, and just chill. Take this time to let your mind wander a bit. Think about whatever you want and enjoy the daydreams. You are using this time to deliberately NOT use any willpower. As such, you will recharge your willpower reserve. I've found that if you do this for 30 minutes to an hour at the end of your day, you will feel much more zeal and energy for tomorrow than if you used that time for something productive. Give it a try for a few days; especially after busy ones. I am sure you will like the results you see.

Conclusion

Balance in life is absolutely crucial to success in college. If one part of your life is malfunctioning, other aspects will suffer in turn. So if something seems to be "off" in your life or you are feeling overwhelmed, see if you can find a fundamental area of your life that may have been neglected, such as the amount of time you spend relaxing, socializing, or doing something you enjoy that *isn't school related.* Even if these things, or other possible imbalances (such as sleep deprivation) seem completely unrelated to the problems you are experiencing, looking at your life as a whole and correcting the life-imbalance can be at times be more fruitful than attacking the problem directly.

Chapter 8: Exercise

The Exercise and Academics Interaction

I know, I know. The last thing you probably want to hear from anyone right now is that you need to exercise and that it's important. We all know this. We were all taught this stuff since we were babies. And yet miraculously very few people (especially college students) take the time to exercise regularly. There are so incredibly many benefits to exercise – benefits that can also help you as a student as well. In short:

- Metabolism speed up (which can result in fat burn)
    - fat burn
    - makes it harder to gain weight
- Fat burn (no freshman fifteen)
- Strength and endurance progress
- Heightened focus on classwork and increased ability to

problem solve

- Increased libido
- Improved physique and muscle tone
- Sleep better at night
- Helps to mitigate stress (reduces cortisol)
- Helps with balance issues in life
- If you don't, you will pay for it later in spades
- Enhance willpower and work ethic and self-control

So really, it's a matter of just deciding to exercise on a regular basis, the benefits outweigh the risks. All these benefits can be yours if you are willing to put in a little effort at the gym or on the pavement several days a week.

How to Create a Plan for Exercise

I could talk for hours on the optimal exercise plan and the best possible fitness model for a wide variety of people. But this is a little beyond the scope of the book unfortunately. What I can say though is that 3 days a week of higher intensity exercise at minimum is fantastic and will yield many of the benefits listed on the last page. It could be cardio, such as running on the dreadmill (yes, I spelled that correctly) or playing a sport with friends. It could also mean weight lifting for an hour on each of those days. Anything that makes you sweat and smell nasty. Put these days and times into your weekly schedule and stick to those appointments! Make a habit of going those days. This way you won't base going to the gym upon how you are feeling that day. If you choose to start an exercise program, it has to be an absolute 'must' to stick to it. You go every day you planned to on your schedule whether or not you feel like it. I promise you, if you make a long lasting habit of this (longer than 4 months), you will see changes you didn't think you could ever see in yourself. You will feel different and carry yourself with a new sense of pride and confidence. There is no greater high on the face of the planet than knowing you've changed yourself for the better. And exercise is just one of those ways you can achieve the level of performance from yourself than you've ever dreamed. Go out and kick ass!

Make a Goal

Create a goal for yourself. So many people go to the gym without any sort of plan or direction that they want to take. They amble about, going from machine to machine with basically no weight on it, or won't try all that hard. It's as if their progress depends only on a factor of time spent in the gym rather than the effort put forth. A muscle only grows and progress is only made if you are working. It's called "WORKING out" not "hanging out" or "instagramming out." Take the hour you are in the gym to genuinely work. You owe it to yourself to see incremental progress, and the only way to achieve incremental progress is by pushing yourself further than you have before. Do that consistently and you will see results beyond even what you expected.

Your goal could be to lose weight, to get shredded, to look more toned and in shape, or something else. But let's also set a "WORKING Goal." A working goal is a different type of goal than what most tend to set. While most goals are set on the premise of an outcome or some end that you'd like to achieve, a working goal is a goal that allows you to actually feel progress in the moment of duress. It's a goal for effort, and not about a result. You don't always get your results and it can be incredibly demoralizing when you don't. You lose the confidence to keep going and putting in the effort when no change or progress seems to be made. The way we change that mindset is with a working goal.

What is a Working Goal?

A working goal is a goal that, when things hurt, you can reflect and draw upon in order to keep pushing yourself. It makes you see that you are making progress by the very nature of you actually putting in the effort. They are only based on how much effort you put in and are completely devoid of external circumstances. Here are a few examples of working goals, but be warned, some may seem a little strange.

-Having a t-shirt with a back soaked with sweat within an hour in the gym.

-Not leaving the gym until you have visible armpit stains without having to lift your arms

-Do 5 different lifts/exercises, four sets each exercise, and each set goes to failure.

-Run 3 miles on the treadmill with a goal of not walking more than n-times.

-Push for one more rep every set. Make a goal for number of reps and beat it often.

-Go 1.10x further in cardio activities than you did the last time you did said activity.

Working goals essentially cater to the human need for quick gratification of effort when willpower is lower than average. This is a marshmallow you can have now AND have at the end of the experiment. It makes you feel like what you are doing is something meaningful and something small that is pushing you to your long term goals. The idea is that you can feel like you have accomplished something just through your one time effort. Because, even if you don't keep up the habit, you have stretched your willpower muscle and that will make more possible for you later. The cool thing is, working goals can be applied in a variety of venues in life. See where else you can use them!

Gym Tips for Success: As with most things in life, things tend to get worse before they get better. And that is when people start to quit; right before the real progress begins and the lasting change that they seek is starting to take form. If you set out to exercise, resolve to be consistent. This consistency is what is going to give you the strength of habit when you can't will yourself to go when you've had a long day or life has gotten harder. This is a decision that needs to become a "MUST" because otherwise you will be tempted to do what your emotions tell you when you really want that donut or you really don't have any more to give that day. If you push yourself even when you don't want to, that is where all the growth and progress is.

Chapter 9: How to Destroy Any Exam

Admittedly, the proposal of "how to destroy any exam" is somewhat loaded. There are no easy "Ace The Exam With Only Three Hours Of Study Right Before the Exam" systems out there, and the ones that claim they can do this with a sufficient degree of success are usually incredibly bright or they are particularly gifted in that subject domain. But if you are like myself or like the 90% of other students currently enrolled in college, acing a test takes a good deal of work. So this section is dedicated to how to prepare for an exam efficiently not only in the few days leading up to the exam but throughout the semester so you aren't left wondering "Why did I not spend more time studying?" after you receive a non-passing grade.

At the outset of the semester…

Figure out when the first exam is going to be and what will be on it. If the syllabus doesn't state the contents of the first exam, you can ask the professor what will be on it roughly. They won't be able to give you exactly what it's going to cover, but because they likely have taught the class before they can give you an estimate.

Throughout the semester...

As you are studying and taking notes on both class and the book, maintain an easy to read glossary of important information that you suspect is exam material. This should be separate from your usual notes. Usually it should contain key points that the professor makes or that the book highlights. Then before your exam, make sure you review this glossary thoroughly.

There is also the obvious necessity of persistent and thorough study habits that must be maintained throughout the semester. Make sure that you aren't forgetting material along the way. Review old material often to keep yourself fresh. This way, you will not need to cram and you are far more likely to do well as your brain has had a significant amount of time to fully internalize the material. You WILL forget some of the material and that's okay! Just do everything you can to retain as much as you can as the semester progresses.

The week leading up to the exam…

Its game time now. You've got a solid week or so before you stride headlong into a big portion of your grade for the course. Up until now you've kept a solid set of notes, have been reading the book, and have been going to class consistently (right?). This week is meant for tying up loose ends in your understanding and practicing problems and questions. There are several things that one can do this week to ensure success that are tried and true.

Figure out on day-1 what it is that you don't know

yet that you need to know. Make a list. Spend a few days learning this material to the best of your ability. If there are still bits you don't quite understand, seek out a peer for help. If they also are lost then both of you should schedule some time to drop by your professor's office. Leave no stone unturned and leave nothing to chance here. Who knows what's going to be on the exam, so the more you understand fully the better off you will be. And if you take time to talk with the professor, sometimes they will give you hints as to what will be on it! Definitely make use of your professor or TA's office hours the prior to an exam. Be sure to schedule enough time to study EVERY SINGLE DAY leading up to the exam.

Occasionally there are old exams posted on the department or your professor's website for you to make use of. If not, ask a more senior peer if they have an old exam. Even better if it's from the same professor. Study them thoroughly. Why? Because professors will often recycle questions, and because the format of the exam will DIRECTLY MIRROR the exam you are about to take. Get used to the format and style of the questions on these old exams and you will be incredibly well prepared.

Lastly, if your class is in the field of the sciences, it is not enough to learn the material or just memorize it perfectly. You have to be able to apply it. This is where I made a huge mistake early in my college career. I thought that if I memorized the material well enough, I can oh-so-simply apply that to whatever the exam threw at me. The hard lesson that it took me about two years to learn was that to do well on science, math, or technology tests YOU HAVE TO BE GOOD AT SOLVING PROBLEMS QUICKLY! I cannot emphasize this enough: DO AS MANY PRACTICE PROBLEMS AS YOU CAN GET YOUR HANDS ON. And furthermore, make sure you are doing them correctly. Once you know how to do a certain kind of problem, move on to a new type. Don't belabor or over-study problems you know how to do already! It will vastly enhance the efficiency of your study if you do this.

Just before the exam

You know that person who still has their head in their notes with 5 minutes to go before the test is passed around? You know the guy/gal beside him who tells them "you know you're not going to be able to learn anything now, right?" The first person got it right. The second is the person who didn't study at all, is going to fail, and is voluntarily announcing this fact and their own anxiety to the rest of the class. Don't be that second person. Be the first. And the reason I say this is twofold.

For one, every minute you spend learning and relearning, the more likely it is that you will find something that might just answer one question you didn't think would be on the exam, and that answer will be fresh in your mind BECAUSE you were studying minutes before the exam. Additionally, by studying just before the exam, you engage in a psychological phenomenon known as "neural priming."

Neural priming is an effect of taking a long-term memory and bringing it briefly into your working memory simply by thinking about it. What happens is that the neurons in your brain will be charged, or "primed" so that when you think about something related to that long-term memory, the long-term memory will be more easily remembered. This is using the subconscious to your advantage. But how does this apply to studying just before the exam? By doing so, you are triggering your long-term memory neurons to fire, and in doing this, all those memories (read: things you've studied) will be "on the tip of your tongue" even if you aren't consciously aware of it.

To optimally use this effect and get the most out of the time before the exam, start your last minute cram session one hour before your exam. Any more and you may risk losing willpower and tenacity when it comes to actually taking the exam. This is especially true if the exam is long. Just make sure you are studying a solid mix of what you already know and some of what you don't know.

During the exam

There are a plethora of test taking strategies for differently formatted exams, such as multiple choice, fill in the blank, short answer, essays/proofs, etc. that you can find on the internet. I highly encourage you to do so! But the one oh-so-simple thing that works on every single one of these formats that makes the most difference in people's scores is thus: ANSWER EVERY QUESTION!!!!

This may seem obvious, but there are just so many students that do not answer every question EVEN WHEN THERE IS NO PENALTY FOR TRYING! If you write nothing for a question you are guaranteeing yourself a zero. Swallow your pride and fears of looking stupid and pick up as many points as you can! The worst that can happen is that you don't get anything. "Pity points" are a very real thing, and some professors/graders give them more or less generously than others. But the worst that can happen is you get nothing for your lackluster answer. The more correct information you have on the page, the better your grade.

This also goes for when you are short on time. Be aware of the 5, 10, or n-minute mark (depending on the duration of your exam). Use those last few minutes to answer anything you haven't answered yet. Give these questions the highest quality bullshit you can muster and you will be rewarded. Again: NEVER LEAVE AN EXAM WITH A BLANK ANSWER ANYWHERE!

A second tactic that is also of critical importance and isn't emphasized enough in test-taking strategy guides is: READ EVERY QUESTION BEFORE YOU START THE EXAM. This is another instance of using neural priming to your advantage. You will subconsciously remember the questions you have read, and as you progress through the exam, you may find that one question statement actually gives you the answer for another question. Additionally, by reading all the questions beforehand, you set your brain to work on all of them. By the time you get around to each question, you may be able to more easily think of an answer!

Lastly, make sure you write in a clear and organized way where it is required. Having good organization and thought flow can make even the most incorrect of answers seem acceptable. This takes advantage of the fact that profs and graders grade incredibly quickly and will often not review your answers line by line. So if your answer LOOKS like it was well thought out, you may just be given the benefit of the doubt. On the other side of that is a threat. If your work is disorganized albeit correct, you may be prone to losing points anyway simply because it LOOKS like it should be wrong. The person grading your test is human and thus can't be perfect grading machines for 300 exams straight. Some can, but that is rare. Just make sure you aren't on the wrong side of a grader's frustration or fatigue. Keep your answers tidy and organized.

The moment you get your grade back

Double check the professor's math when they calculated your points. It's amazing that more people don't do this given how often small miscalculations are made, and very rarely is such a miscalculation to your advantage. I've seen cases where ten percentage points on a final were lost because of an addition rounding error which resulted in the student being given a B+ for the whole semester when they deserved an A. So ALWAYS, ALWAYS, ALWAYS, double check the math!

Another thing you need to double and triple check is whether or not you were graded fairly and the grade on each question is correct. Professors and graders make mistakes too. They are human after all, and they also tend to grade quickly (See: Get the Edge in Grading). So make sure there are no obvious mistakes on your profs/graders part. Be sure that these things are addressed the same day you get your exam back. If you don't, the less likely your professor will consider altering your grade and won't think you are cheating by changing your exam.

Note: One way you can buy yourself more time to review and make sure no mistakes were made against you grading wise is to take your exams in pen if possible. If you come back a few days later stating that the grader/prof made a mistake, they won't be as easily able to accuse you of altering your exam.

Going forward

Study the exam and try to redo the questions you did not receive perfect marks on. Make sure you learn from your mistakes and never make that same mistake again. Odds are those questions or similar questions will find their way onto your final or another exam, so it's best to know the solutions going into the next exam. If possible, find or ask for a blank copy so you can retake it on your own time just to get the material down perfectly. Optimally, after a week of receiving your grade, you should be able to take the exam over again and earn a perfect score AND be able to take it more quickly.

Chapter 10: On Failing a Test or Assignment

So. You've just failed your test. You get back your answer sheet and all you want to do is burn it, go home and get your mind away from the misery and humiliation by hopping on the internet or video games, or some form of beverage with high alcohol content. But I challenge you instead to think. What's it gonna be from here on? Are you going to wallow in your misery and pretend it didn't happen just to protect your pride? Or are you going to own it, learn from it, and do what most others *will not* so that you can achieve what others *cannot?* Don't get me wrong with the above statement. It is okay to have negative emotions in a time like this. The trick is to not let them stick longer than necessary. We will discuss below a few simple ways to strategize, make productive changes, and get some of that energy and zeal back so you can go at it again next time even harder. Strike now while the iron is hot.

So you've already reviewed your exam for point calculation errors, and have noted what questions you got wrong (see: "How to Destroy Any Exam"). You feel the pang of crappy emotions and you are worried for your grade for the entire course because heaven knows that there is only one exam aside from the final and a handful of homeworks or projects that will only lightly buffer your grade. You may be in a class where that test could very well fail you for the entire class. If this is the case, you MUST ABSOLUTELY follow the simple rule which we will go into in the next chapter: Do not quit the class under any (academic) circumstances. But at this point you may be wondering: "What can I do?" I'll let you tell me.

Make a List

Write a list of 15 things (it must be at least 15!) that you can do from now until the end of the semester that would help you be successful to utmost degree. There are so many resources available to you, so why not tap into them?

Here are five things to get you started

1) Use professor's office hours... all of them. Beat other kids waiting by being there first.

2) Do all suggested problems that aren't graded. If there aren't any recommended, ask the prof!

3) See if there's a tutoring center on campus that you can visit. Usually they are free of charge.

4) Make friends with the smart kids

5) Find additional course material (e.g. lectures from other profs, online tutorials, etc.)

6) .... 15)

Now that you have your list of 15 things, I need you to go through this list and find the two things that if you could do them in the next day or so would radically help you the most in achieving the level of success you desire. Strip away all the other items that may seem easier or less helpful, and focus only on the ones that will make all the positive difference no matter what it takes.

Now the most crucial step: TAKE ACTION!!!! Put those two items on your schedule for the next day and COMMIT TO DOING THEM! No excuses. If you want to see radical improvement, you have to get out of your comfort zone and do something radically different. Because after all, what you have been doing has not gotten you the level of success you want, and doing MORE OF THE SAME will certainly not make things better. You have to do something different, and it starts within 24 hours. Make it happen and go after it as if your life depends on it... because it does.

Modeling Success

This very much echoes bullet 4 on the suggested list; making friends with the smart kids. These students have shown that they are doing something right, and only a handful of them can get away with being constantly naturally gifted. Success leaves clues. Many students who are successful have a "system" that they live by -- a system that has served them well, and is helping them achieve the success that you would like to see for yourself. Talk to these students. Ask them what it is they do to prepare for a test; how they study; what they read; what their work ethic is like. They will be honored especially if you are a total stranger, and most people would be willing to help you! After all you just paid them an implicit complement. They are going to be a bounty of useful resources. Use their experience and don't try to reinvent the wheel. What they are doing works so use their ideas and strategies. Likely, if you experience setbacks while doing these things, those people may know how to help you overcome them! Odds are they have faced similar difficulties. Humbly model their success, you shall also be successful. But also feel free to make changes and customize their approach to what works for you! Someone may come up to you one day and say "Hey, you did really well in that class! That's awesome! I was curious though, how did you go about attacking it? It is one of the hardest classes we have here." Always return the favor.

What to do When You Aren't Doing Well in a Class

There almost certainly will be a class in college in which you will struggle to get by with a C. There may even be classes where you run the risk of failing or are already failing and are at the point of no return. So, as before, I ask you the question: "What are you going to do?" Are you going to quit? Give up and try some other class that fits the requirement? Complain about how you were treated unfairly or how the class was terribly taught and organized? Everyone else does this. They moan and groan, and when the going gets hard, they quit. They simply stop trying all the while possessing this sense of entitlement that they somehow deserved better and were robbed of it; playing the victim. But you aren't like everyone else. You are reading this book because you want something more out of your education and you are doing your damndest to make a name for yourself. You set out at the beginning of the semester with a purpose. You set out to do as well as you could in your classes, and learn a skill in each. While things may look bleak right now and you may be permanently failing that class, you still aren't finished yet with that goal.

While you may not be failing the class, you aren't doing as well as you'd prefer or you are below a certain required grade cut-off. What can you do? I'll tell you what I commonly see when people start to struggle in my classes. They stop trying and stop performing at their best. They stop going to class and turn in fewer assignments. They don't study, and they sure as hell don't stop by my office to ask for help (I'm pretty approachable and I don't smell all that bad). They just sabotage themselves! Plain and simple. Why? Because they want to minimize the emotional stress and pain of doing something that makes them feel inadequate. They avoid the work of the class and anything to do with it because it simply causes them pain.

There are always a handful of students who, when faced with a tough situation such as sub-par performance or even risking failure, turn around quickly and do the best work I have ever seen out of them. They take personal ownership of both their circumstances and their emotional state, and they make the most out of their situation. They go to class. They ask for MORE homework assignments for practice. They seek resources. In consequence, they become even more successful than when they started, AND they quickly built the determination to succeed in that class. They realize that when life gets harder, it's time to hustle, not give in.

So what can YOU do to make the most of your situation? You have a goal of doing as well as you can in this class, so what can you do to hustle? As before, make a list. It's time to tool up and pool your resources. List 15 things you can do to improve your current situation, pick one or two of them that you could act on immediately, then COMMIT TO THAT ACTION WITHIN 24 HOURS. If you do this simple process, I can promise you, within a few weeks you will be head and shoulders above where you are at this very moment both in your class and emotionally. You will feel the empowerment needed to persevere and you will have resources to get you to exactly where you want to be. Note also, that this tactic generalizes to life in general. Try it out outside of school and you will see what I mean!

Making the Most of a Failed Class

Most who fail a class midway through the semester stop going to class. They stop caring because they feel they have nothing more to gain, and lots of time wasted on class they have to retake anyway. But this is where so many students get it wrong! Most of the time, they will have to retake the class again and they know it. They also know they struggled and didn't quite make it the first time. How can they expect anything different the second time around when they haven't learned all they could the first time?

Sure, you can drop the class if you see it necessary, but what advantage is it to stop going to that class altogether? You still have something to gain, and that's where everyone goes wrong. Hence the following rule:

DO NOT QUIT GOING TO CLASS.

Under no academic circumstances should you stop going to class and participating in it completely! If you have failed or dropped, **think of it instead as a risk-free opportunity!** You aren't graded formally on anything anymore, so who cares how bad you screw up? In fact, you should ask if you still can be graded informally so you know how you can improve! After all, you may need to retake the class, and if you can replace the class with something else instead, you will essentially be wasting all that time you already invested. So make the most of your investment and finish what you set out to do. Don't be like everyone else who gives up when life knocks them down. You are here to grow, to learn, and to build character and inner strength. All these things vanish for quitters.

Chapter 11: Becoming Incredibly Resourceful

The single most valuable skill that a student in college can possess is resourcefulness. At many points in your life you will be provided with many of the tools you need to be successful. In school, these take the form of books, lectures, notes, Google, professors, etc. In life after school, you *might* have your peers, your significant other, your parents, and Google, if you are fortunate enough. But despite having a wide array of people and tools available to you, more often than not they will be completely insufficient in aiding you to reach your goals. Heck, even in some classes all the usual resources you have at your disposal might not help because they all suck! So what do you do? This is where being resourceful comes in handy. It is at the point where no one is there to help, where you have no tools to your name, that you have to either find a way or *make* the way. This is where your resourcefulness will be most of use to you. So if we are fortunate enough to cultivate this skill of resourcefulness early, we will always have the ability to pull ourselves up by our bootstraps when there is little external help available.

In this chapter, instead of exploring a set of resources available to you given particular life or academic circumstances, we will discuss how to seek out resources and how to have the confidence to use them.

A Day in the Life of a Resourceful Person

Let's start with an example. Suppose you want to get a job after college in a particular field. You have heard up until this point that interviews for this job are brutal and they ask all sorts of penetrating, analytical questions that fully test your knowledge. But as it turns out you don't have the faintest idea of what kinds of questions will be asked, let alone how to answer them! But one thing you do know for sure is that you want that job more than any other job and that you are willing to do whatever it takes to get it.

Where do you start? You know that interviewing is going to require answering tough questions, so it would make sense to figure out what kinds of questions will be asked. But how do you do this? Google, right? But what else could you use? What other resources are available to you? Hey wait a second... Didn't Joe apply to that job last spring? You could shoot him an email, no? And you suddenly recall that one of your professors also worked in that industry for 20 years and was a hiring manager. You could stop by during his office hours and talk to him about the job and get some insight! Also, you realize that you have built a good deal of professional rapport with him. He could also serve as a reference when you apply! So you keep that in the back of your mind.

So after Googling, sending an email or two, and visiting this professor, you now have a very good idea of the types of questions that will be asked in that interview! But now we have another issue: You still have no idea how to *answer* any of those questions. Heck, you barely understood the content of the questions in the first place! You think for a second that perhaps you are not cut out for this job and you should find something better tailored to what you know already. But then you recall that this job pays $70,000 per year starting, has full benefits, and has a great work environment with flexible hours. You remember *why* you wanted that job in the first place. You also know that you have a good deal of skill in what you have learned in college so far. So you decide to *find a way* to answer those interview questions, even though you have no clue how at this point.

So back to Google! You decide to devote a few hours a day over the course of the week to just understand what the questions are asking. You learn in the process all the stuff you *don't know* and therefore now have an idea of what you *need to know.* Furthermore, this gives you an edge because you now know what you are looking for when you start trying to learn the material required to answer those questions. So you Google some tutorials, but everything you find is about as clear as mud. You think that it may be time to call it quits, but you decide that there may be other resources that you haven't considered yet. You decide to wait a day or two and focus on other things. On day 3 you decide to get coffee at the campus coffee shop, and you overhear a couple students studying the exact same material you were trying to learn via Google. You are beyond grateful that you did your research, otherwise you wouldn't have noticed them!

You take a deep breath after grabbing your mocha-schmocha-frappasomething and approach them. “Hi! My name is ______. I overheard you two talking about thermonuclear astrophysics. I have this interview at XYZ inc. but I am not as familiar with the interview question material as I need to be. I was wondering if you could tutor me on this material. I can certainly pay you for your time!” The students look at each other in surprise that someone would so spontaneously ask such a favor, but they agree to help you. Over the next couple months, you learn not only the material you needed to know, but you also mastered every single interview question that you could get your hands on. You get the job in turn, and you live radioactively ever after.

The above is a somewhat silly example of what a truly resourceful person looks like. While the story above may seem relatively unrealistic, I posit it only seems that way because most people don't think like this. Most don't have the drive or audacity to do what the person in the story did, so this mentality feels completely foreign. Most people start off well with some initial zeal for their goal, but they get stuck somewhere in the middle. We will detail the qualities and mentality of resourcefulness in the following paragraphs so that if you ever find yourself stuck, you can always find a way to proceed. Every one of the following traits are seen in the story above, so to help with internalization see if you can find them!

Leveraging Your "Why"

We have discussed in Section A the importance of having a "Why." Like in the story above, knowing your "Why" and keeping that in mind throughout all your efforts is going ensure that you see it through to the end no matter what. Giving up halfway because it gets hard is equivalent to giving up on your "Why." It's a hard truth, but a truth all the same. A resourceful person knows their "Why" at all times. They know what they are after and they are determined to make their "why" a reality. Otherwise, if they didn't know their "Why" they couldn't ultimately reach their goal quite simply because it wasn't clear to them what they were after. Know the reason for everything that you are doing. Know exactly what it is you are after and don't count the cost of making it happen. A clear vision of your future is crucial as it will aid you in stepping out of your comfort zone and seeking the resources you need to make that vision a reality.

Breaking Things Down Into Steps

Not a soul going to see how to get from where they are to where they want to be at first. For the bigger problems in life, it never is that straightforward. Most of the time, we can't even break the path from point A to point

B into smaller bite-sized chunks. Why? Because we don't have a clue how to even get started, let alone blaze a straight and narrow trail to the goal. So how are we to break things down into steps when there's really no path there in the first place? Actually, there is a path, but you have to start building it first even though you have barely a vague idea of where you are going. That's where the steps come in. As you start building this path, the next step you need to take next will reveal itself. More often than not, you won't be just given the next step. You will be given the *next several* steps. Perhaps you will be given a few choices for what next course of action you should take. Some may take you closer to your goal, while some may take you further (see the next paragraph for how to deal with this). But what is important is that you keep progressing with your end goal in sight. Much like driving a car in the fog, you can only see the next few meters in front of you, but in order to see further you must first go further. And occasionally, you will hit a clearing where the fog is less dense, allowing you to get to your destination more quickly.

The Shotgun Approach

This is one of the defining characteristics of a resourceful person. Not only do they know what they are after, they come up with many little ways to help themselves get there. Like in the story, the first roadblock that this student encountered was not even knowing what questions would be asked in interviews. Likely after a little thought, they noted that there were three resources at their disposal. Instead of trying one of them and hoping to get good results, they tried all three at the same time! Much more efficient, no? While you may end up needing to do more work on the front-end, you won't be spending any extra time trying one thing after another. A resourceful person is one who finds and explores many options simultaneously in order to get the result they want.

If Trying One Approach Doesn't Work

So often it is tempting to keep trying the same approach to solving a problem, or using the same resources even though it doesn't serve you well. "The devil you know is better than the devil you don't" as the adage goes. After all, you already put so much time and effort into your current approach. People naturally feel that changing methods will make all of that effort a waste. And because of this inclination, trying an entirely new approach is never the preferred course of action. A resourceful person knows that there are many ways to do any task, and that if a person wants to see different results, they must do something different. Consequently, this idea also generalizes well to life as a whole. If you want something different than what everyone else has, you must do what nobody else is doing. This leads nicely into the next point.

Audacity and Humility

This is the single largest sticking point for people when it comes to resourcefulness. If you ask people to list all the tools, people, and resources available to them to solve a given problem, often enough, the ones that involve talking to people are the ones that are omitted from the list. It is usually why professors are lonely during office hours even though half the class is failing. People for whatever reason cannot humble themselves long enough to ask for help when they need it. If you have ever been in a car driving with someone who won't stop and ask for directions no matter how lost they get, you know this to be true. Or potentially, people fear being rejected when they ask for help. Resourceful people acknowledge that they need help at times and will not hesitate to ask for it even in the face of possible rejection. To be honest, the worst that another person can say is "no" and more often than not, it is a very polite "no." They know that another person may be able to get them to their goals far faster than if they struggled alone, and it is well worth the risk of rejection. Even the great Sir Isaac Newton, being the conceited jerk that he was, said once "If I have seen further than others, it is by standing on the shoulders of giants."

Resourcefulness as mentioned before, is far and away the most important skill that a college student can have. If fully honed and mastered in the five ways mentioned in this chapter, there is very little that can stop you from achieving practically anything in life. If you don't know the way right now, you can always find the way even when it seems like there is no way.

Chapter 12: Getting an Edge in Grading

In my entire experience as an undergrad who talked regularly with professors in different fields, and being a Teaching Assistant with around 60 fellow TA's, I have learned one thing that is almost completely universal: Everybody hates grading. The only thing that varies is to what degree each person hates it. Think of it this way: a professor/TA/grader will have to grade each and every assignment you turn in throughout the semester. If this is a science or math class, this may be the equivalent of thousands of problems per semester; thousands of the same problems with the same mistakes that are given the same feedback for hours on end. Grading sucks.

You may be sympathetically nodding your head, or

perhaps thinking "what the heck do I care? It's your *job* after all!" While this is certainly true, I am not complaining for the sake of pity. I am instead giving a brief glimpse into the grader's world so you can take advantage of it. Knowing now that nearly everybody hates grading, you can tailor your graded work to the mindset of the grader. This sounds far more sociopathic than it really is. In fact, by implementing the following strategies, you will be helping both yourself and the person grading your work.

Neat Work is More Correct than Sloppy Work

Having graded thousands upon thousands of homework assignments and exams, I can certainly say that the level of organization and clarity that I see on students' work runs the gamut. Many students have a good degree of organization and clarity in their work, but there are others that have scribbled out paragraphs written in pencil, writing that gets pushed into the margins and suddenly shrinks 28 font sizes, scratch work in several different places, and solutions that look like they came out of a shotgun. Graders want to minimize the amount of time that they spend grading. So to see work like this will be mildly irritating because they have to take extra time to work through the chaos. If the grader can't figure out what the student was thinking in a reasonable amount of time, they will simply give points for what little they could find. And that's in the best case! I've known graders who give next to *zero* points for badly written work. Either strapped for time or simply pissed off that they have to grade longer because of a student's lack of organization, graders can easily justify slapping a zero on that work (no matter how correct it may be) and move on.

So what's the moral here? Whoever is grading your work is going to do so quickly, and the more easily they can read your work, the more ably they can give you points. So before turning in your assignments, make sure they are scratch work free, scribble free, and neatly written (if it is to be done in handwriting). Make sure that your work makes sense when you read it to yourself. Bonus points if you have a friend look over it just to make sure it *flows* nicely. You want your work to be as easily readable as humanly possible, even if it's wrong at times (graders will catch your errors no matter how you try to disguise it). As the name implies, "pity points" and (extra) partial credit are given when the grader is feeling generous. Thus, by having cleanly written work you are helping both the grader and yourself.

Develop a Reputation for Good Work Early

Unless you are taking introductory level courses, most of the classes you take will have less than 50 students enrolled. This may seem like a lot, but surprisingly, this is still considered a "small" or "medium" sized lecture at many schools. The class is more intimate and it's far easier for the students to get to know everybody. It is also much easier for the professor to get to know everyone as well. Professors are surprisingly observant and in such a small class they get to know you and your work fairly quickly. If you are in a larger classroom, then the *graders* are going to get to know your work fairly quickly. And believe it or not, because of this, your work has to make a good first impression.

Recalling that nearly everybody hates grading, it is certainly reasonable to expect that your grader is going to try to finish as quickly as possible. They will not spend too much time on any one part of a student's work. Sometimes they will simply glimpse at it just to make sure the student gets "the gist" before slapping it with a grade and moving on. This is more rare, but does happen to various degrees. But in order to just glimpse at a student's work and grade it quickly, they have to have reason to believe that the student is indeed correct without them having to scrutinize every detail. How can a student achieve this on their end?

At the outset of the semester, the student must be bent on submitting their best work. That is, a student must have cleanly written, correct, and for all intents and purposes, flawless work. What this does is it establishes to the grader that the person who wrote that work does a good job on average. Graders do not forget good work or its author! And because of this, the grader learns that they can trust you to get the details correct, and more often than not, that your work as a whole is generally correct. If you do good work early and often, you are far more likely to be forgiven when your work is sub-par on occasion. However, a word of warning: if you make a good first impression with your work for the first several weeks only to let it slowly get worse as the rest of the semester progresses, you will lose your edge with regard to this strategy. Like with people in general, you may find someone charming at first only to realize with time that they aren't all they seem. Similarly, you may dislike someone extremely the first time you meet them, but over time they grow on you. So for this strategy to be ultimately successful, you need to be turning in solid work more often than not. It doesn't have to be flawless, but it does need to be good *frequently*.

Going Above and Beyond

This isn't necessarily about simply putting more effort into your studies, but at the same time it is. This is about making sure your professor *knows* you are putting in the effort. Why does this matter? Because semester grades aren't as cut-and-dried as it seems. One thing that is substantially different about college grading as compared to high school is that professors generally do not have people keeping tight tabs on their grade book. The syllabus certainly will list how you will be graded in a very detailed way, including how much of your overall grade each assignment will be worth and also letter grade percentage cut-offs. But at the edge of each of these cut-offs is invisible wiggle room. Say, at the end of the semester you have an 89.45% overall grade; just shy of an 'A'. The professor, with their amazing amounts of grading freedom, can decide whether or not they want to round up or round down. The question that comes to their mind is "does this person deserve an 'A' ?" Of course, it is up to the professor how they use this discretion if at all. But in my experience most professors do make this type of decision every semester. Moreover, the amount of wiggle room they are willing to use is quite subjective and based on whether or not they would feel 'okay' about rounding up or down (most wont round down to the same extremes they may round up). So throughout the semester it is your duty to convince them to round up in your favor.

But how exactly do we 'convince' professors to round up? Quite simply actually. Show the professor that you are putting in your best effort no matter what your grades look like. There are many ways of doing this.

Suppose that at the end of class the professor decided to take time to review old material and half the students decide to get up and leave. If you are one of the few who stay, you will be remembered for doing so.

It is remarkable how few people actually use the professor's office hours. I know that I and many of my peers maybe see one student a month. So be different from the rest of the class and go to office hours! You can talk to the prof really about anything that you are having trouble with or perhaps homework questions. If you aren't struggling in the class whatsoever, you can still go to ask how you can improve your assignments or determine if your answers are on the right track. Make a habit of going to office hours at least once a week. This is the single biggest way to show the professor you care about the class and about the education you are receiving.

If the professor offers extra credit, always be sure to at least try it. If you find yourself at that 89.45% at the end of the semester and you haven't even attempted to do the offered extra credit then why should the prof have mercy?

Another useful way to make yourself stand out as someone who is trying to succeed is simply to participate to the best of your ability in class itself. (See: Using Class Time Wisely)

Almost certainly this short list does not cover the numerous ways you can convince your professor to round up at the end of the semester. The key takeaway here is the question: "what can I do to show the professor I care about my success in this class?" If you keep this in the back of your mind in every class you take, you will reap the rewards of this tactic.

Tailoring Your Work to the Professor/Grader

Even in the little things you do in your life, such as brushing your teeth, you have a method you follow when you do these things. You may not be entirely aware of it, but deep down, you do things the way you do because you think it is "the right way." Otherwise, we wouldn't have enough confidence to walk out of the door in the morning. We'd need constant instruction for simple things such as how to use a fork and spoon. This "correctness mentality" runs deep and it is defined explicitly by how each of us interacts with our environment. It is absolutely no different for professors. Professors all do things the way they do because they think their method is correct to some degree. Occasionally, and depending on the subject, they may feel their way is "the only way." Professors certainly try their best to remain objective while grading, but at the same time they are human and are not impervious to the subconscious processing that occurs within the correctness mentality.

We've all had that English class where written papers were assigned asking for your interpretation or opinion on a certain matter. Perhaps it was even a research-based class where everything you said needed to be cited in some way. In such a class, you may have had the experience that no matter how well you wrote or how well you documented your paper, you still couldn't earn high marks on anything. As it turns out in cases like these, the correctness mentality as we mentioned before may be playing a role in how you are graded. So how can we overcome this occasional yet inherent lapse in objectivity?

From the title of this section, you already know the answer.

But what does it mean exactly to "tailor your work to the professor"? Quite simple. Because the professor has their own unique way of doing things, they grade students' work with the subconscious criteria of "how well does this match what I know to be correct? That is, how much is their work like my own?" So to tailor your work to them is to make *your* work resemble the style and format of *their* work. Your work should not, of course, be a blatant copy of their style. Merely, your work should *resemble* theirs. Nearly all professors and instructors have a Curriculum Vitae on their website that is chock full of links to papers they have written, including their thesis/dissertation. They may have given you excerpts of their work in class too! Read a few of them and take to heart how the professor writes stylistically. If you can incorporate that style into your work, you will earn favor with the professor in terms of grading. This is of course assuming they are the ones reading your work. If they are not, then tailor your work to whoever is reading it if possible.

It should be noted explicitly that I am not suggesting that you shouldn't have you own style in your assignments; you certainly can! We are just looking for subtle ways to *incorporate* your professor's style, such as vocabulary, paragraph and sentence length, etc. The aim is to work with their style while not compromising your own. It is entirely up to you if or how this is accomplished.

Picking Writing Topics with the Grader in Mind

This is very similar to the strategy above. Like how professors have a set of methods by which they do things, they also have a framework for how they see the world. That is, they have opinions and interests. So when picking a writing topic, it is usually not wise to pick something you know that they are morally opposed to or simply hate. Instead, if you can pick a topic that aligns with your interests *and the interests of the professor* you are more than likely to be on your professor's good side when they grade your paper. If you pick a topic that is contrary to their interests or opposes one of their beliefs, they are naturally going to be more critical and exacting while grading. It is not at all that professors all have some sort of vendetta against you because of your opinion. Rather, it is simply the same subconscious knee-jerk reaction you would feel if a person openly disagreed with you! Even if you could handle it with tact, you still would feel negatively about that interaction. As before, we want the person looking at your work to be in a good emotional state when they grade it. If you are unsure if a topic is of interest to them or is off-limits, simply talk to the professor after class. In most cases, for longer written assignments, they will require that you get your topic "approved" before you get started. This is a great time to get a sense of how the professor feels about a given topic. If all else fails, have them help you find a topic! Odds are they will not pick one they dislike (they have to read it after all). If all else fails, you can always check out their publications for ideas. If you manage to find a topic that is related to their work, they are more likely to read your paper with a positive mindset... that is, unless your work contradicts theirs of course.

Chapter 13: Building Habits

Habits. We all got 'em. Though when people think of habits, the first thing that usually comes to mind is “smoking” or “overeating” or “checking your phone constantly.” Most of the time what comes to mind is something negative. In fact, a habit is just something that you do consistently and repeatedly, either good or bad. If you think about it, most of our lives are governed by out habits. Very little of what we do in a day is actually well thought out and deliberate. With little thought, you just *act.* You get up in the morning and immediately fire up the coffee maker. You drive to work or campus the same way every day. You exercise after your classes five days a week. You eat your meals at the same time. You go to church on Sundays. You brush your teeth every night... et cetera. Virtually everything you do in a given day is governed by your habits. But of course they aren't limited to daily tasks and things you do. They are also involved in how you interact with others and yourself, such as how you talk with your friends or even how you think. Your thoughts, your actions, and your words are all governed by the habits you have built up until this point. So consider it this way: you are what you repeatedly think and do every day. It's in knowing this that we derive power to become successful in anything we wish to achieve.

Not a single person on planet earth that is a self-made success achieves their success overnight. Olympic athletes don't just show up in some random country every four years thinking "Maybe it would be cool to try some of this figure skating stuff out." Successful businesspeople don't just grab a business license and chill on a recliner until their franchise makes money. This all seems obvious doesn't it? But naturally, with media the way that it is, we are inclined to believe that these people all had a miraculous gift or a "stroke of genius" that made them substantially different from everyone else -- a gift that took them from a 'nobody' into an instant celebrity. The truth is, the media doesn't have the time to cover the *thousands of hours* these people put into their craft; the time they spend practicing, their sickening work ethic, the little things they do every day. But indeed, it is in these little things they do consistently every day that makes them successful.

Success is not a monumental event but the culmination of a vast collection of little habits built up over time. A skyscraper is not built of one giant hunk of concrete laid suddenly. A skyscraper is built of thousands of smaller bricks, laid carefully and precisely one after another. Thus, success comes from all the small steps you make toward your goal every single day. And by making these little steps a habit, by making them a part of who you are, you will naturally build the way to your goals just by living.

Start Small and Build Up Naturally

Suppose there is a habit you want to cultivate, say, reading over all the lecture notes immediately after class for example. Instead of saying to yourself "I am going to study the lecture notes for an hour every day for the rest of my life" you could tell yourself simply "After lecture this week, I am going to review the lecture notes for 10 minutes." And then, the next week you can decide "I am going to study for 15 minutes after class." You can likely see where this is going. By starting small, the habit you want to build doesn't seem nearly as much of a feat that requires an insane amount of willpower. This is the beauty of what is called "Habit Stacking."

To effectively stack habits, you first start with a vision of where you want to be; what habit you want to cultivate and keep over the long run. Create the image of the habit you will cultivate in vivid detail, asking yourself questions such as "how will this benefit me and my life?" Once you have fully visualized the habit and yourself doing it regularly, think to yourself about the first small step you can take to achieving that habit. The trick here is to make this step really small, easy, and achievable such as the one mentioned above. Then commit yourself to doing that one small step as soon as possible. Make a habit of doing that one step for a few days to a week. After you feel yourself firmly grounded in that tiny little habit, see if you can up the ante a little. Change the habit or increase something about it slightly enough for you to barely notice the difference. Then commit to this slightly altered habit for a few days. Continue the process for as long as it takes to get you to your goal that you first visualized. You will be utterly astounded to see how fast you get there. Moreover, you will start to see the benefits of your habit along the way! There is even a chance that you may wake up one day and not even realize that you got to your goal a long time ago!

It should be noted that this method takes time. Because of the slow step-by-step nature of habit stacking, it will require some patience to see it through until the end. So throughout the process, if you aren't quite seeing results just yet, keep going at it! Keep in mind that visualization you did earlier and decide to keep progressing with your habit. Once you get to your goal, you will be so thrilled and feel a sense of accomplishment.

To Kill a Bad Habit

Not too surprisingly, this can work much in the same way as habit stacking. If you have ever watched a tree being professionally cut down in a residential neighborhood, you know that they don't simply chop the tree at the trunk with an ax or a chainsaw. They start by climbing the tree and taking down the individual branches before chopping it down at the trunk. By doing this, they prevent damage to homes and property, and usually don't kill anyone in the process. Likewise, you don't start killing a bad habit by taking on the whole tree, err I mean habit, at one time. You can end a bad habit by taking it down one branch at a time.

Much like the above, the goal is to start small and build up. Say you want to stop eating junk food. You know that you typically eat three snacks a day, including potato chips, ice cream, and a candy bar. One way you could start cutting away branches here is by replacing just one of your snacks with a healthier one, such as fruit (fruit preferred because it's the closest healthy thing to a candy bar). Committing to replace just one snack with an apple instead for a couple weeks will set you on a path to success. After those couple weeks, see if you can replace another bad snack with a good one. It's even better if you can eliminate one of the bad snacks. In general, the rule is to start small and build up over time. This works for nearly any habit (sans some addictions) and can be employed in nearly any facet of your life, including your studies.

Killing a Bad Habit with Replacement

The example above gave an outline of ending bad habits with replacement. All too often it can be more of a challenge to remove a bad habit by simply abstaining from it completely. Suppose you watch 4 hours of television a day and you want to stop. Odds are if your routine is to come home and plop down in the armchair to watch the game and this has been your routine for years, it will be next to impossible to simply stop watching television outright. One thing that you can do to counter this effect in addition to habit stacking is to replace the bad habit with a more productive and beneficial one. The best effect comes when you replace the bad habit with something similar but less detrimental. For the example above, instead of watching television for four hours a night, you could decide to read a book or online news articles for 30 minutes prior to flipping on the tube for the remaining 3 hours and 30 minutes. Replacement along with working in small barely noticeable steps is one of the best ways to kick any habit that doesn't serve you.

Don't Give Up Ever!

More often than not, changing a habit can be challenging at times. Not always will it be so, but there will often be a stumbling block placed in your path on the way to success. You may find that you skipped a day during your habit building (such as going to the gym... i.e. Leg Day) or in some way you failed to achieve that one small step. This is okay! This will happen from time to time. It is so important to not get discouraged by one setback or two. If you encounter a setback, decide that the next day or the next chance you get that you are going to get right back on track! When building a habit, I have heard many people say that once they start, occasionally things get worse. But from those same people, of the ones who persevered anyway all agree that things get worse before they get better. In fact, it is not uncommon that once you get past that roadblock or set back that things really start to go incredibly well! So keep that in mind as you are working toward anything: Things get worse before they get better. And when they get better, they often get really damn good!

Keep a Calendar

I've found it particularly useful to plan out on a

calendar each of the little steps I will take. That is, I will write across the entire week the small step I will be doing every day. Then when it's time to change to the next step, I will write that on my calendar. This I've found to be useful because it keeps me honest and on track. That way I can actually plan out in advance how long it will take me to reach my big goal habit. If you can plan out each little step in advance in this way, it makes progress toward your goal habit measurable.

Limiting the Quantity of Habits You Are Changing

The old adage "A dog that chases two rabbits shall catch neither" rings true when it comes to habit building. If you try to change too many habits at once, you will find yourself struggling with each of them in turn. Pick a number of habits that you want to build and make sure that it is no greater than 3 or 4 at any one time. My sweet spot is around 2 habits. Any more and I won't progress on any of them. Any less and I get impatient. Two for me is sustainable. If you think that working on 3 or 4 habits at a time is sustainable for you then go for it! But if it proves to be too much, decide to cut back a few of them. Whatever you do, do not quit all your habits altogether! Just find your habit building sweet spot and try to see them through till the end.

Conclusion

At this point, you may be considering a vast number of habits you'd like to cultivate that would help you in your studies or perhaps in your life as a whole. Write them down! Pick out a few of the ones that will make all the difference in your life, and commit to starting small on each of those. By employing the simple steps above and remaining steadfast if the going gets tough, you will be living more productively, efficiently, and happily.

Section C: Prepping for the Future from Day 1

Chapter 14: Tailoring Your Education to the Job You Want

Life, it seems, is frequently organized as a set of stages. You go to school. You go to college. You get a job. You get married. You have kids. Your kids have kids. Your great-great grandkids have kids, you retire. You die. Always a series of succinct stages, seemingly disjoint or perhaps related only because one follows after the other. Not so surprisingly, when in the midst of all these stages we treat them as such and act accordingly, even though we *live continuously* through all of them! And often, we find ourselves at the precipice of the next stage completely unsure of what to do with ourselves. While some things are naturally unpredictable at times (such as having a child) in most cases we can see the next milestone on the horizon. Moreover, we can see the smaller milestones in the not too distant future. You'd think that knowing what's coming would be helpful; that it would give us an edge so that we are prepared. While it does theoretically, it's not how we do things! Most times we approach the next stage of life like a skydiver rapidly approaching the ground. A skydiver who thought that, given his situation, he may have been better off with a parachute. We always see it coming, but we often don't act until it's too late.

While stages are a useful way to compact the continuum of life into more manageable bits of information, it really doesn't serve a person well to operate this way. It also surely doesn't serve you in this "stage" of higher education.

The Mindset and Angle of Attack

Because life is a continuum, we certainly should act as such, no? There is always something coming toward you in the not too distant future and it doesn't care if you are ready for it or not. So to avoid hitting your next milestone as hard as our unfortunate skydiver friend hit the pavement, it is necessary that we see what is coming, that we plan, and then act on it in advance. As for most things in your life, you either do things passively, living in the moment, or you invest your time for tomorrow's betterment. Each of course has an appropriate time and place, but in the midst of a long-term time investment such as college you simply cannot afford to be just "putting in time."

Often enough throughout college, students forget that they are building something. I mean, this is the first time they actually had go out and put in years of effort into something with little guidance. Up until now, it has been almost sufficient to go to class (i.e. in high school) and do what the school had prescribed in order to be successful. They have thus built this psychological causation of "going to class and following the suggested guidelines made me successful in the past, and this situation is similar to the past, so therefore doing that same thing will likely bring me success." This would be true, but there is one thing that is lacking... GUIDELINES FOR YOU TO FOLLOW. Everyone in college is after something different. Each major is tailored to a specific industry that is frequently changing. Even your department can't keep up at times! Additionally and more importantly, you aren't *given* guidelines anymore. You have to *seek them.* Why? Because there is no blanket advice or guidelines for a set of people who are all chasing something different. So while taking classes is important to ensuring your success, you also need to be thinking about what lies ahead for you.

Your time now has been committed to your investment. Rather than "doing time" for years, wouldn't it make more sense to find ways to maximize your return?

The end return

So why are we doing all this anyway? Why are we to slave away at textbooks and lecture notes for four-plus years? Answer: It's completely up to you! Most who graduate college naturally will seek some sort of employment. Some go on to starkly-higher education. Some people opt to do something completely unrelated. In any of these cases, someone else is vying for the same role you are. Therefore you will need to market yourself well in order to secure that role.

Regardless of what someone tells you, when you attend higher education, you are there to build a product that you will take to market. It just so happens that this product you are building is **yourself and your skill set**. We all know that the businesses that provide the best value consistently to their customers are usually the most successful. So, you being a business trying to market...well...yourself, to a customer that goes under the guise of "employer", wouldn't it make sense to try to sell the best-valued product out there? In the following sections we will discuss some of the ways we can best do that. As I mentioned before, there is no blanket step-by-step guidelines that one can give that will help every college student be successful on an individual basis. Instead, we will seek to help you *build* a set of guidelines for yourself that works specifically for *you* and what *you* want to achieve post-college.

Entering the Job Market

The last days of the last semester wind to a close. You are graduating the day after your last final and you are beyond ecstatic. The whole future awaits you, with so much potential, and now that you've paid your dues, it's time to cash in! You pass all of your exams and finally graduation day arrives. The commencement ceremony comes to a close. You let out a cry that can be heard for miles, "I MADE IT THROUGH COLLEGE!!!" But then you realize and quietly say to yourself, "Oh shit, I need a job don't I?" This sounds a lot like the parachute guy! So to make sure that this isn't you come graduation, we will discuss in this section how to tailor your education to landing a great job.

But what's better than landing a job post college? Landing a job you actually WANT. Note that this is different from your dream job. Different only in that it's a job that you can enjoy doing for the time being, and a job that can get you to your dream job.

What do you want to do?

So the first question I have to ask you is: What IS your dream job? What can you see yourself doing 5+ days a week for 8+ hours a day? You may already know what this is, but for most students, they really don't know until they find themselves working all the jobs they DON'T want. So do a little digging! Even if graduation is 4 years away, the earlier you can figure this out the better. Disclaimer: This might go against everything you have ever been told. That is, "you can start job hunting and worrying about all that by your senior year." This is true, but only on a microscopic point. You can start *applying* for jobs in your senior year. The search begins as soon as you have a ballpark idea of what industry type you want to work for. The ACTION you take will follow immediately from that.

Once you have a vague idea of what you want to do post college, start searching for jobs that sound appealing to you. Take lots of notes on what you find. List the pros and cons of each position. What do you like about it? What is completely repulsive? But the most important thing you need to really take notes on is EXACTLY what a person does with that job title every day. Find jobs that look appealing overall, and then figure out exactly what a person with that job does. This is done with two goals in mind: A) determining if it is a good fit for what you want to do, and B) to gather information pertaining to what you have to ALREADY BE DOING prior to even applying. This last bit is crucial.

Solving the "Need Experience But Need Job for That" Dilemma

Now you may be thinking "But how am I to do a job without actually having the job?" We will get to that in a moment. But let's first talk a bit about the dilemma facing college kids entering the workforce fresh out of school. I am sure you have heard the Catch-22 "I need experience to get a job, but to get experience I need a job." And for those who are less lucky, because they are desperate, they end up in a position that is completely unrelated to what they want to be doing. Or worse, they move back in with Mom and Dad. This problem has been worsening over the last decade or so, with more kids unemployed upon graduating than ever before in history. Thankfully, it is a problem that can be easily be circumnavigated with a little effort. The key is to get the experience WHILE STILL IN SCHOOL.

The above is a trite and cute answer to our dilemma. But of course HOW one is to go about doing this may be exactly what you are wondering. The sections that follow will give you a starting point.

Internships

This is far and away the most frequently cited way of getting experience before entering the workforce. It's also not one that should be shrugged off so easily. Having an internship in your field of interest does a variety of things for you and your resume, such as:

1) Getting your foot in the door at a company you may want to work for

2) Building rapport with people in your field (See: Networking)

3) Recommendations from those who work in your field (Absolutely, critically important)

4) Job experience in your field that you can list on your resume

5) Getting an idea of what you may be doing or would want to do post-graduation

6) Working on a variety of projects and problems which you can talk about in interviews

7) Gives you a chance at leadership, depending on the field.

8) Gives you confidence that you can do the work you're studying to do

9) Applies a bit of your classroom knowledge (usually only a little bit of it, mind you)

10) Gives you credit for school depending on your program

11) Sometimes a bit of cash

What to Look For in an Internship

THIS IS REALLY IMPORTANT! Every job that you found earlier in your search is going to have a list of responsibilities and tasks associated with it. You researched the job duties of each position in depth because your goal is to get experience doing those things before you even apply! So like your job hunt browse around the internet, your college department, and the Career Services Office at your school. See if you can find an internship (preferably paid) that looks as much as possible like the jobs you researched earlier. The more experience you get in your internship doing the job you *want* post-graduation, the better your chances of landing that job. So if this is something you'd be interested in, start your search for an internship now! There are places that will hire college students as early as their sophomore (2nd) year! And if you're still a first-year, LOOK ANYWAY! Pooling your resources now will make the search later a bit easier.

Oh, and while actually working your internship, there are just a few things you need to do in order to reap every benefit that is on the list above:

Work Your Butt Off!

For starters, you need to do the best damn job you ever have in your life. It doesn’t matter if you are paid like crap; that’s not why you are there in the first place. If you get a job done, go ask your manager for more work! Find things to do, and make use of every second you are working. Work all the time you work. Don't waste your boss's and your time on idle chitchat with co-workers. Tell your co-workers to go over to someone else and ruin their career! You are there to make a name for yourself, and you need to work like every little thing you do or *don't* do matters (within reason. You likely won’t be stalked by your boss too much). If you do the best work you can, it will give you list items #1, 3, 4, 5, (part of) 6, 7, 9, 10, 11.

Doing More Than Required Begets More Experience

To get #'s 6 and 7, after you have established a solid work reputation for yourself and your boss takes notice, you can ask if they could put you on different projects or give you different tasks. They usually will be surely glad to oblige! After all, most employers want to help you be successful if you demonstrate that you are willing to put in the effort. Not to mention, if you ask to do more good work for free, who can refuse that? They may even give you leadership responsibilities, but that largely depends on your field. Doing this will establish a broader portfolio of experience in your field. Then you can list on all of it on your resume and talk for hours about in interviews (but don't literally do that last part).

Building Rapport

Lastly, to get #'s 2, and 3 on the list, you not only should you do outstanding work, but you should also make a point to build rapport with your co-workers, your boss, and any higher ups that you can. This is different from making friends. You are building a professional relationship. This means that you communicate and work well with others in your job environment, and you readily contribute to the common cause of the company. The people that know your work ethic and the impact that you have had thus far in your internship will be sure to remember you. They may even serve as additional references or offer you a job! Yes, this does actually happen in outside of Disney movies.

Overall, an internship can benefit virtually any college student in any field. Since you have been looking into post-college jobs in which you'd be interested in applying, you can thus through an internship and be able to check off a few of the job requirements that you need. You also can potentially gain experience DOING ALREADY what these positions entail from day to day. If you pick your internship right and do an outstanding job at it while using the tips mentioned, you will be in *insanely* good form when it comes time to apply and interview.

Getting an Actual Job

One viable alternative to an internship is getting an actual job. You may be a similar situation as me in that you have little choice *but* to work in order to pay the rather large part of your tuition that your loans don't cover. So an internship isn't going to fly because the pay is bad and you need the cash. But all is not lost! To much disbelief of many, there are certainly positions in the job market that are in your field, and that will hire you on a part-time or even full time basis for decent pay. Companies may not necessarily have an internship program in place for a variety of reasons, but they may compensate for that by hiring college students, hoping they will stick around longer than a few months. If you can land an actual job in your field you will gain *nearly all* the benefits of an internship.

A few words of caution, however. While these jobs exist, they are harder to find than internships. They also may not provide you with the same breadth of experience or networking opportunities. This is because management has hired you to do a small set of tasks and exposing someone in your position to a variety of projects is not a priority. In an internship, they often make a point to give you experience. In an actual job, they don't necessarily. While even if this is the case, you can still take initiative and get involved in other projects to increase your exposure! If you follow the same guidelines that were mentioned in the section on internships, you will have all sorts of stuff to put on your resume.

If the Job You Get Is Not In Your Field

This is actually okay, believe it or not! There is good experience that one can get even while working at Taco Bell. For instance, I worked at a coffee shop for most of high school and all of college. It paid well and gave me the hours I needed so I could afford school and a beer every now and then. I was worried that being forced to work there would rob me of the experience I could get elsewhere, but as it turned out it was one of my greatest strengths when I interviewed for a Software Developer position after college. I was able to describe in detail a few of the problems I faced regularly while working that job. I was also able to describe times I was put in brief leadership roles and the obstacles that come inherently with them.

These stories (and believe me there are many in customer service) were enough to impress my interviewers. Even though I was interviewing for a software developer position after college, my experience at the coffee shop was an asset rather than a liability! They actually helped me get the job! So if you get a job not necessarily in your field but you do the best work you can, you can surely spin your experiences to your advantage.

A little more warning: If you don't have ANY job experience in your history whatsoever, this is a red flag to many employers. Inversely, if you *have* had a job or jobs for much of your age 16+ years, this is typically seen as a good thing. At bare minimum, it's not a bad thing to have a work history, but it IS a bad thing to NOT have any. I had two friends who incidentally experimentally verified this point. Both had virtually the same good grades and coursework history but one had held a job for 6 years in customer service and the other did not have any work history at all. Both sent out dozens of applications. The one who had the work history heard back from probably 1.5 times as many companies. This isn't a perfectly controlled accidental experiment, but it's certainly enough to raise an eyebrow.

All in all, having some sort of work experience is of critical importance. Though, it is certainly much better to hold a job that pertains to your field of study and is similar to the job you *want* after you graduate.

Starting or Getting Involved in a Project

This is a great way to earn some experience in a direct and nearly fully customizable way. If you go to a bigger school, odds are either your department or a related one will have projects in which you can involve yourself that *directly relate to the job you want.* If you are in engineering, there are always students trying to design build things. If you are in social sciences, there are many research studies in which you can participate. If you are in education, you can get involved in tutoring on campus. If you are in English, see about working for your school newspaper. The list goes on and on and you are limited only by your resources and resourcefulness in this manner. Be sure to ask professors in your field about different projects that are available to you. They would be happy to help!

You may be at a small school or at a community college where projects are hard to come by. In which case, you have to get a bit creative! Since you looked into jobs that you might apply to post-college, you now have an idea of what your future employers are looking for in a job candidate. As such, you can *create* a project based on those job descriptions! Here are some examples:

If, say, you are looking into software engineering and you know that they work in teams to build software solutions, see if you can get a few friends together to brainstorm apps that you may want to develop and eventually sell on some mobile platform. This will tally up as leadership, and you would thus have the repertoire of *having already worked on a team* in software development.

If you are an English major, you could start by writing blog articles or articles for online news sites. Such sites may want to see a portfolio of your writing, but on occasion, they work by article submission. That is, they pool articles from a variety of authors and pick the best one. This will build up a *working portfolio* that you can use when applying for jobs and other freelance work.

If you are an electrical engineer, and you know that

the job you want will have you designing and maintaining in-home security systems for home owners, you could build a team to work on a small scale project that sends notifications to a person's phone when someone has entered the engineering lab. Like with software engineering, this will tally as leadership and working the job you want *before you even apply.*

The above tiny list is just to get you thinking in the right direction; thinking like someone who does the job they want before they get it. This is the key element to doing projects while in school. Your work should be applicable to a real-world scenario in some way. And if you are at a loss for ideas, talk to your friends and your professors. Your friends will likely have a lot of ideas, but they may lack the *drive* to start them. If this is the case, you can give them a helpful nudge by beginning the project with them. Your professors will *always* have ideas, but they lack the *time* to start on them. Professors will have the time, however, to advise you and give you tips on how to get going.

Project resources

There are also a variety of tools on the internet that you can use to find project ideas. They often serve as a "freelancer hub" where people list small jobs they need done and how much they will pay someone who does them. There is literally no limit to the types of projects that are available. Everything from graphic design, writing, website programming, music production, gardening, you-name-it, are posted on these sites. Additionally, if you for some reason can't find a project that matches your skill set or can't find something you would be interested in doing, you can post a job you are *willing to do* and you can charge for it! These sites include but are not limited to:

-Freelancer.com

-Elance.com

-fiverr.com

-guru.com

-upwork.com

-patch.com

The idea with these sites is not necessarily to make money (while that is a pleasant corollary), they are there to help you build a portfolio of work-related experience; experience that you can take to market when you graduate.

Note that even as you work on these projects, you can always take a step back and determine if this is something you even want to be doing. If it is not necessarily, you are always at liberty to change things or even change majors. If you think that you will have wasted your time and effort as a result you are mistaken! Like having an unrelated job, every project you do that is even semi-work related will give you something to put on your application. All the problems you solve and the obstacles you overcome will be brilliant fodder for when your interviewer asks you what you do for fun. Every experience you have is always in some way applicable to what you do in the future. This is true for life in general; not just while job hunting.

Clubs and Competitions

In addition to projects that you can find on campus or create yourself, you can also look into the wide variety of clubs that your school offers. Even in your department, you may be able to find such clubs. But as with projects, they should be as applicable to your field of interest as possible. Suppose you are a Performing Arts major. You could join the school choir or audition for the next musical. Those clubs will be highly applicable and are something you can add to your portfolio of work before you apply to jobs. If it is applicable, it is fair game.

That isn't to say that you shouldn't involve yourself in other clubs or activities on campus that are *not* in your line of work. If you have the time for underwater basket weaving club and it's something you want to do, I say go for it! While not directly applicable to your field, you may be able to gain some leadership experience if you participate for long enough (then it IS applicable!). Leisure and fun activities, while they may not help your chances directly of landing a job, will certainly benefit you in other ways. Having fun in college is important!

A word of caution though: try not to involve yourself in a club (or even a sport) for the sole reason of having random extra-curriculars. Engage yourself in meaningful activities. That is, if you don't want to being doing a particular activity AND it's not pertinent to your future job, then DONT WASTE YOUR TIME! Random extra-curriculars are important when you apply to college (even that is debatable), but after that, they have little meaning because they have nothing to do with what you will be hired for post college.

Competitions in your field are another way to get experience and build a work portfolio. For example, the computer science department that I was in offered students the chance to participate in team programming competitions against other schools twice a year. One was a massive 24 hours straight, and the other was more like 5 hours. I had friends who did both competitions every year since they were freshmen, and thus by the time they graduated they had 8 competitions under their belt. What was even better was by the time they were seniors they were ranking very well in these competitions. They took their competitive programming history with them to interviews and landed themselves jobs at places like Amazon and Microsoft. Such competitions are a great way to build experience. And even if your school doesn't participate in many competitions, you definitely can find competitions online in many cases. It's almost amusing when you see competitions like "high speed article writing." If people can be good at something in a measurable way (even subjectively), odds are you can compete with it.

Research

This sort of follows from projects and in a way research is definitely a project that can be beneficial to your work portfolio. It's especially useful and can take you even further if you manage to get research published. For further details, read the research section of "Entering Academia."

For Those Considering Grad School

If for some reason you are as crazy as myself and are seeking ever-higher education post-graduation there is a lot you can do to prepare yourself. The list is short, but the effort you have to put in is where the “a lot” comes from. It all really depends on what flavor of degree you want to get in graduate school. This section will cover the (very) basic necessities of what you could do to enhance your chances at getting into a fantastic graduate program.

For PhD's

A PhD is a research degree. You will have to do all the coursework of a master's degree student and then some. And then you have to turn around and contribute original work to your field via your Thesis/Dissertation! Since much of your time after you complete your classes will be devoted to research, the hiring committee will be looking for your ability to actually do publishable research in your field.

For Master's Degrees

These degrees are not as focused on research, but rather on a series of classes that you have to take to better yourself in a particular field. The program requirements vary by school, but in nearly every case that I have found, the focus still lies on coursework. In some programs, you will have to do some form of "Master's Thesis." This type of thesis however need not be original research. It can take the form of a project or a paper. A project may involve creating something, like a performance portfolio or a robot that performs some task. A paper usually involves learning a specific topic well enough to be able to write and talk about it intelligently in a "thesis defense" setting. You may be able to do original research for your master's project, and if you do, your professors will love you for it!

For Other Degrees (Such as those in medicine)

These programs vary in what they will ask you to do in order to get your degree. In many cases, you will at some point have to fulfill some sort of "residency requirement", which essentially is working part or full-time in your field under supervision. Since these programs have a focus on "doing something" rather than research, that is where you need to put your focus while in undergrad. And internships or some form of field-related work are an absolute must if you want to be competitive upon applying.

The above degree type synopses are extremely generalized. If you are interested in entering academia once again post-college, you should make a point to research specific programs at specific schools and determine what is required by each. This should be done to even more depth than if you were looking for a job.

Graduate schools are very hard to get into on the whole, and it's definitely not a cakewalk once you are there. So by doing some research beforehand, you can adequately prepare yourself for this undertaking by doing as much as you physically can while you are still in undergrad. The grad program research is maybe 5% of the effort. The rest is actually DOING what it takes to make yourself competitive when applying. This is the part we will address in the next couple paragraphs.

Research is Gold

In nearly every case, students applying to graduate programs of virtually any type can benefit from doing research while in undergrad. Doesn't matter if you are a pre-med student, an education major, a mathematician, or musical performance major, you can benefit from doing research. The only thing that varies is the amount to which it benefits you and your applications. It ALWAYS will look good on your applications. Especially if your research is original work and published! If you have publications in scholarly journals while you are still in undergrad, you will have ten times the opportunity as someone who doesn't.

While you can always come up with research ideas on your own, it is often far better to seek the advisement of a faculty member who has already built themselves quite the research legacy in their field. They likely have hundreds of ideas that they haven't acted on yet. And many of these ideas may be accessible to an advanced undergrad such as yourself. If you built rapport (See: Networking) with your professors, they will be happy to assist you. They may even include you as part of their current research! This is great because they publish often and will likely sign you as a co-author when they publish your joint work. Even if you don’t get a major role in their research, they still should credit you anyway. A publication where you aren't the primary author is still a publication under your name. It is even better if you are the primary author and the professor only advised you. If you can get one of these research relationships underway and if you are diligent in your work, you will most definitely see results for your efforts. And if you do well in your role, your professor/research-advisor may ask you to help with their next project as well! At bare minimum, even if you don't end up with a publication, you can still get a fantastic letter of recommendation that attributes to your ability to do research, so you really can't go wrong here.

REU's

REU, or "Research Experience for Undergraduates" programs are opportunities that typically take place over summer vacations with the aim of research and publication. In these programs, you will likely be working in a team at another university on a given set of research topics determined by faculty. There the faculty will guide the teams and help them rapidly produce solid research that often is publishable. REUs are highly intensive and require you to put your nose to the grindstone for hours and hours a day. Its hard work, but well worth it. They also give you weekends to just have fun on your own. These programs can last for a few weeks to a few months. They are hosted by many universities around the globe, and they often pay your travel expenses. You are usually paid a stipend for your work that will cover basic living expenses (plus a little extra beer money). Even if you don't get publishable results, you still can list the REU on your applications and have it be incredibly valuable.

On the True Importance of Good Grades

If you plan on applying to graduate programs of any kind, you MUST ABSOLUTELY have good grades. Grad programs are ultra-competitive, admitting on average 20 applicants out of 200 or 300, and often GPA is the first thing they use to determine who gets rejection letters/emails. While it is necessary to have high grades, it is not sufficient on its own. That is, if you have a good GPA it won't damn your applications, but if you don't, it certainly will. If you have a GPA of 3.00 or lower by the time you reach your senior year, you may want to consider getting a job and then going back to school later. Adult learners have far better odds because faculty know they work five times harder than the average incoming college student even if they had average grades way back when. Though it should be mentioned that if you have an OUTSTANDING GPA in the 3.90+/4.00 range, your odds of getting into a well-ranked grad program are much higher.

Standardized Tests

In America, most accredited schools require that you take the standard Graduate Record Exam (GRE). This exam is a souped up version of the SAT/ACT you took to get into college. It covers exactly the same material (Reading, Writing, Mathematics) by and large, but it is more in depth; especially with the math section. Like with GPA, having decent scores will not hurt you but having terrible scores will. So practice as many problems as you can get your hands on!

Depending on your graduate program, there may be a GRE Subject Test that you have to take as well. For example, when I applied for graduate school in math, I had to take the Math Subject Exam. So check well in advance at the schools to which you want to apply to determine if you have to take a Subject Test. These exams are DIFFICULT! They are also curved. So a raw score doesn't matter as much as how you did compared to everyone else, which is reflected in the "percentage" statistic when you receive your scores. This is the percentage of how many kids you beat who took the test on the same day you did. Make sure you study incredibly hard for these exams if you have to take them. Take every practice test you can find and every simulated exam that is offered on the internet.

As for all standardized testing, it takes time to grade and return to you. So air on the side of caution and take your exams no later than October of your senior year. This will give plenty of time to evaluate where you are applying once you have your scores returned. If you take them really early, you can opt to take them again if you feel the need.

Though I should note: if you did not do well on your Subject Test, it is not the end of the world! Many schools to not care about them as much. They use them often as a school-wide statistical formality. I had made 23rd percentile on my math GRE, which is straight up shameful (you're expected to score in the 80th percentile in my field) and I was accepted at a few different schools anyway. If you are applying to Ivy League or other Big Name universities, it matters far more; it's another application statistic they can use to weed out weaker students. This does not apply as much to the standard GRE. On that one you need to do well.

Letters of Recommendation: The Most Valuable Asset

These are the single most important aspect of your application! You need to have professors or professionals who are well regarded in their field attest to the high level of work that you do. Your grades and test scores will never tell the full story. Your research will to some degree, but in the absence of a solid research portfolio, what can an admissions committee depend upon to determine whether or not you are a good candidate? This is where networking is crucial (See: Networking)! You need people who are familiar enough with your work to be able to say something meaningful about it and about you as a student.

You don't *just* need a specific number of recommendations (usually two or three), you need to have GOOD recommendations. If a professor isn't too familiar with your work, all they really can say is something like "Well, she/he seems like a hard working student, and she/he got an A- in my class one time." This is the type of recommendation letter that you DONT WANT. Unfortunately, it is also the one that admissions committees see the most. Why? Because many students never put in the time to network properly or to talk to professors. So make sure that you have made a name for yourself well in advance. The earlier you determine you want to apply to graduate schools, the earlier you can pick the professors you want to recommend you (without telling them yet), and the earlier you can start showing off.

When you set out to ask for recommendation letters, don't just ask "Professor Xyz, could you write a letter of recommendation for me?" You instead should ask something like "Professor Xyz, could you write a GOOD letter of recommendation..." Most professors will not turn you down when you ask, but if you ask if they could write a GOOD letter, that changes things a bit. They will be more inclined to say "no" if they don't think they could recommend you well. A bad letter is worse than no letter. So be sure you have 5 to 6 professors in mind before you start asking just in case you get a few refusals.

Also, just one thing worth mentioning: Be sure to thank your recommendation writers! Not a simple vis-a-vis "thank you", but an actual typed and signed letter. This is professional courtesy for when anyone professionally does you a favor, and it's a good habit to start early. Plus, you may need to use them for recommendations in the future!

While professors don't expect a “thank you”, they are definitely tickled pink when they get one!

Teach/Tutor

Since many graduate programs will require its students to teach actual classes or lead recitations, it’s a good idea to get some teaching experience beforehand. Admissions committees will also look favorably upon your application, not to mention, *because* this role is part of the job requirements. They want good teachers too! So if possible at your school, see if you can tutor via their Learning Support Center or some equivalent. Campus Learning Support Centers are always looking for good tutors in a variety of subjects, such as math, the sciences, writing and reading, psychology, business, and many others! And if they don’t offer a tutoring position for someone with your expertise, there are always opportunities online as well! Having some teaching/tutoring experience will pad your application quite nicely if you can find the opportunity.

Diversified Applications

While you may have done well to ensure your application is as tight as possible, complete with fantastic test scores and a great GPA, unforgettable recommendations, and a solid research portfolio, it is always a good idea to apply to a wide range of schools that vary by quality. This mirrors what you likely did when you applied to college. You can pick a few "reach" schools that are harder to get into, but be sure to apply to several mid-range schools where your chances are better and some lower end schools as a fall back. Aim for around 6-10 schools in total. The more schools to which you apply, the better your odds!

Grad School Apps Ain't Cheap

Applying to schools is downright expensive! The prices range from 50$ to 120$, so you have to budget accordingly. Not to mention, standardized exams aren't free either and can vary from $75 to $150. Just for some perspective, I spent about $800 for all my applications. If you include the tests, it was just over $1000.

Above we went over a few tips that will help you get in to grad school, but we did not go into much depth on what work is actually involved once you are there. While it merely looks like "just more college" it is an entirely different world. Many of the strategies outlined in this book may still work, but most of them go out the window. You need a sickening work ethic and a drive that is unparalleled. It is an absolute "must" to be incredibly resourceful and you have to develop the ability to do the seemingly impossible on a regular basis. An entire book could easily be devoted to just *surviving* graduate school. But if you are tenacious, persistent, and hard-working, graduate school is definitely something that can benefit you and your career. If you decide to go this route, the above tips will help you get there.

In conclusion

As I mentioned at the outset of this chapter, life is not a set of different "stages" per say, but rather a continuum. And college, being a brief part of that continuum, should be met with strategies that prepare you for the day you graduate. And if you do even just a few of the things that were mentioned in this chapter to prepare, you will be far better off. You will not be simply applying at the spur of the moment with little more than a GPA to your name. You will be prepared well in advance. You will be armed with a solid work portfolio *tailored perfectly* for the jobs you are applying to, and all sorts of experiences to discuss when you go to interview.

Chapter 15: The Importance of GPA

By this point you've likely heard the popular adage "C's get degrees." While this may be true in general for even for your particular major, C's will indeed get you degrees. You know, those sheets of fancy paper that you receive after you don the cap and gown on graduation day? But to think about what the degree actually is constructed to be, it is designed to represent the acquisition of knowledge or skill in your chosen area; a certain degree (pun intended) of expertise. So from a philosophical viewpoint, do you truly have a degree of expertise in your field? Or do you have a sheet of fancy paper that allows you to masquerade as if you do? In other words: a lie, plain and simple?

Aside from the moral implications and the mindset of "C's get degrees" there are three main points that we will address here regarding grades and GPA.

1) "Will my future interviewers care about my GPA or my grades in particular classes?"

Throughout my undergrad I was told countless times that my GPA didn't matter as much as college advisors made it out to seem. I was told that employers are looking for someone to fill a job role with someone qualified and my interviewers would not ask about my GPA or individual grades because 'that doesn't indicate job related performance.' WRONG!!!! When I interviewed for a software developer position immediately after I graduated, one of the very first questions they asked me in my first round of interviewing was "What is your current GPA?" I was utterly surprised. Everyone (and there were many) who had told me that an interviewer would not ask such a question was DEAD WRONG. And what's more was then in the second round, they asked me if I had taken specific classes and what grades I got in them! Everyone who had told me employers did not care to see past a person's degree was gravely mistaken.

I had several friends who were graduating alongside me, and I told them of my surprise regarding my interviewer digging into my grades. Most of those I told WERE NOT SHOCKED AT ALL. They all had the exact same experience! So I conclude that this myth is dead enough to be completely disregarded. No more security blanket to hide under; your GPA and grades matter post-degree.

2) "What purpose can GPA serve as a predictor of success in the workplace?"

Well in many ways it doesn't correlate perfectly. That is, a stellar student may be an average employee, or an average student may be a great employee. So why use GPA in the interview process? Let's try to get into the head of the employer a bit.

Suppose John Doe walks into an interview holding a fresh degree in Computer Science, but sports a GPA of 2.8. Not terrible, but not good either. And then his buddy, Steve Crane walks in for the same position holding a solid 3.30. Assume that both individuals are equally well prepared and qualified aside from their GPA. The interviewer now needs to speculate why John has a lower GPA. While his marks aren't terrible, they certainly aren't good either. The interviewer is going to reference his or her own experiences for a basis of comparison; they are going to ask "what do I know about people with a GPA of 2.8?" They may even think to themselves "Well, I had a 2.6, but I was barely sober for half of college..." John's interviewer may have been a straight A student and associates anything lower than 3.2 with laziness and apathy.

This all may seem relatively subjective, but if we look at this as a continuum, it all works spectacularly well and actually has an apparent order. On the right end of the continuum, corresponding to the higher marks in a neighborhood of 4.0, the associations one can make with such a GPA are essentially positive. As you move further away from the 4.0 mark, the number of positive associations starts to dwindle. And when you cross a certain point on the spectrum, the amount of positive association is outweighed by the negative, and that's where you get into trouble come interview time. So the moral of the story theoretically, is that the higher your GPA, the more likely that part of the interview will be in your favor.

I mean, what does it mean to have a high GPA? What does it take to keep high marks? It takes drive, tenacity, a never-say-die attitude, resourcefulness, and a willingness to put in the work when it's needed even if you'd rather be doing something else. So, to put it simply, If you go into an interview with a higher than average GPA and show them you worked your ass off to get there (this last part is key, otherwise they may think you're really bright and that's the end of it), your employer will assume you have many of these qualities, or at bare minimum, won't think you lack them.

Another reason for having a higher GPA is there are companies that have their Human Resources department sieve out applications by specified criteria. Much like your entrance to college was partially based on your standardized tests and High School GPA, companies will weed out candidates by several means and on occasion GPA is one of them. So if for any other reason, there is a need to beat as many other job candidates as possible. And this is even before you are even considered for an interview. Some smaller companies will interview first without HR getting involved and sieve out applicants in this same way. Just be wary.

3) Interview Strategy: Using a High GPA to Your Advantage

As mentioned before, the associations the interviewer has to your particular GPA is entirely based on their prior experiences. But believe it or not, there is a way you can control what those associations are. The two cases outlined above, in the instance you have a high GPA, the interviewer will assume either you are naturally gifted, or you worked hard to earn the marks reported by your GPA. But them thinking that you are intelligent isn't going to get your hired alone. But if you instead show them that you earned your GPA through blood, sweat and tears that will be of more value to them than your wits alone.

How does one do this?

If your interviewer asks you directly about your GPA, do not just give a number and wait for the next question. Instead, you could state even slightly humorously "after much effort I earned a, 3.78." There are a bunch of ways you could rephrase this, but of course be cautious of your audience. This is a small point you can use to your advantage, but it certainly won't hurt your chances if you don't.

Conclusion

GPA is certainly not the end-all-be-all culmination of your college experience and most certainly isn't going to be what get you a job. But it certainly can be used to your advantage in several ways if you indeed have a high GPA. But if you have a low GPA, this my friend, can damn your chances.

Chapter 16: Networking

It was mentioned before in the previous chapter that a college student needs to not only be focused on their present school work but on the future and what lies ahead for them after college. In this section we will elaborate more on one detail that many students tend to forget or end up doing too late in the game. That is, networking.

Everyone after college plans to be going somewhere with their education, be it graduate school, starting a career, or starting their own business of sorts. And in every single one of these situations there is always a need to have references. That is, you need people who know you, your work, your work ethic, and potentially your financial history (in the case of starting a business). It is very true the statement "it's not who you are, it's who you know." And in the event that you don't "know" anyone, you may struggle more than you have to when it comes to getting on your feet post-college. Thus I cannot emphasize enough the importance of having a solid professional and academic network.

Admittedly, I fell into the category of "students with virtually no network" going into my senior year. I knew I was going to try to apply to graduate school in math since day-one of undergrad. I also knew all along that I was going to need at minimum three references for my applications. While I jumped on research and projects when I got the chance, I didn't work with faculty enough for them to truly know the ins and outs of my work. By the time I needed to apply to various schools, I had one great reference, one moderate, and one poor (by "poor" I mean the reference couldn't say very much). I would have had only one reference period if I didn't scramble during the fall semester of my senior year. I had the regret of not having started earlier. Likely, not having three solid references kept me out of my top choice schools. So given this experience, I implore you to start as early as you can to develop your network so you won't run short on references when it comes time to apply to jobs or school or for whatever it is that you need to "know somebody" to do.

Networking as a Habit

I'm sure you have a friend or know of someone who just "knows everybody." If you walk around campus with them, you will inevitably hear hundreds of people say "Hey Joe! How's it going?" This person is the epitome of someone who is well-networked and who naturally makes a habit of getting to know people. They are experts when it comes to marketing their brand; that is, themselves. They are always in the loop with many social groups and many faculty members, and in turn they have an extreme amount of power whether or not they know it. They aren't powerful in and of themselves, but they always "know a guy" who can help them. Their network is what makes them powerful. This is very much how politicians or businesspeople run their lives. They know by themselves they are limited by what they know and the time that they have, so they outsource their work to someone in their network. Most of these people were not born with the natural extroversion required to garner such a wide network. They had to establish *a habit* of getting to know people on personal and professional levels.

While the benefits of having a great network are pretty straightforward, you may be thinking "but doesn't it take a lot of effort and time to cultivate such a network?" It actually takes far less than you think! How many people do you think you interact with on a daily basis? Your peers? Your professors? Your grocer? The person running the Taco Bell Window? Now on average, how long do you spend interacting with them? Of course this will vary. You will of course spend more time with your friends and peers than you will with professors or the dude working the Taco Bell. You will likely also frequently see many of these people repeatedly. Now what if I told you that you could do one small thing in your interactions that will make all the difference to that person and to your network; one thing that most people just don't take the time to do? I'd sound pretty crazy right? Well try this.

Cultivate the Habit of Caring about Everyone

Starting Small

How often is it that when you go to the grocery store and get in the check-out line your interaction is limited to "Did you find everything okay?" "Yup." and you swipe your card and go on your merry way? Since we are looking to build a habit of networking, why not start small with these types of interactions? How could you make this person behind the register feel cared about in those few minutes? You could pay them a compliment on their hairstyle, or an interesting tattoo, or perhaps something they are wearing; any way you can get a conversation started. One thing that I have found to work wonders is a simple "Thank you." But this is different "Thank you" from the one you say when you grab your shit and leave. Suppose the store is busy and the person running the register seems a bit stressed. You can then say "Hey, I know it's really busy today, but I just wanted to say thank you for the work you are doing despite how crazy it is." And if you say this with a genuine smile and confidence, they will feel so appreciated and valued! You may even get a smile back! But don't be discouraged if they meekly thank you in return. They are having a bad day after all.

But it doesn't stop there. The next time you are at the grocery store, see if you can get in that worker's line again. Same procedure here, but this time you already have a little rapport with them (they will likely remember you), so starting a brief conversation with them will be easier. Feel free to share about your own life briefly with them. They almost always will ask "How are you today?" So this is a great chance to tell them that you are doing well because you passed your last exam with ease. Just be sure you don't complain! Because of the rapport you established, they will probably ask follow-up questions. If you keep things upbeat, the person with whom you are speaking will learn to associate positive emotions with you when you show up in their line. You have become a break from the grinding monotony of their job. While it may sound cheesy, after doing this several times, you will have added one person to your network. Not only that, but you have started building the habit of showing interest and caring about complete strangers. You have begun cultivating the habit of skilled networking. You likely have many of these small interactions on a daily basis; none lasting more than a few seconds to a few minutes. Each of these is a chance to get to know someone just a little bit and have them know you! So take full advantage of these little opportunities to grow and to make someone else feel cared about in turn.

Note: If you currently are working in some sort of customer service position, the tables are turned slightly. You now have the ability to make the most of interactions with DOZENS of people. The employee who makes their customers feel the most valuable is always the one that is remembered and sought out the next time the customer wants to make a purchase. This means you get even more practice with repeated small interactions! You get practice in making people feel connected to you.

Stepping it up a notch

Your interest of course lies not only in short interactions at a grocery store. You are interested also in starting to build professional relationships; relationships that can help both you and the other people involved (because you are just as valuable to them as they are to you). Like with the grocery store example, the aim is to make an impression on the people you talk to. You want to be on good terms with as many people as possible, no matter what their role is in your life. So, considering you interact with so many different people and perhaps professors on a daily basis, ask yourself this: "What could I do to build rapport with each person that I talk to?" And believe it or not, it works the same way as the previous example. Just try to get a conversation going! That's all it takes. It doesn't ever have to be a long conversation, just one that beats the usual silence and cold detachment. And by being on good terms with these people, you are at a far better place if you need someone to "pull strings" for you. Often, you will find that people with whom you are networked (even in the simple ways mentioned above) will *want* to help you and will go out of their way to do so. But likewise, you have to be willing to help them as well. This leads to another great way to build your network.

Offer Your Services

You are a multifaceted human being; one with many valuable skills and talents. You are going to school to hone some of these after all. So how many people do you think could benefit from your help? Suppose you are good at physics and the person you are talking to, who is currently working the register at a restaurant, is studying for a massive physics exam that they don't think they will pass. Since they frequent this restaurant themselves, you could ask them if they'd like to meet at said restaurant for a brief tutoring session. While it may take up a few hours of your time, the fact that you volunteered to help them so readily will strike a chord. You may even find out that they are an English major and they can help you on your next essay! Because they are human just like you, they too have a wide array of skills and talents. Not to mention, they probably also have a network of their own. So by helping them, you not only do them a great kindness, but they will also be willing to help you via themselves or their own network!

Building Working Relationships

You may be thinking "That's all well and good, but the dude at Taco Bell may not be able to give me a reference when I need a job." Believe it or not, there is indeed a chance that someone you meet might *know* somebody who can give you a job. Not to mention, this person whom you've befriended to some degree has only positive things to say about you at this point. While there is a chance that they may know someone who can give you a job in your field, we aren't going to bank on it by itself. We need to cultivate working relationships as well. That is, we need to be networked with someone who is familiar with the work you do who can then attest to your abilities when you need a recommendation. The method for doing this, however, does not change in the slightest.

In the last chapter, we discussed that doing a job well while working under someone else's guidance can be the key to a great recommendation. However, you need to already be working under someone for that to happen. Despite what it seems, this is not another Catch-22! You have built up the habit of getting to know everyday people through everyday situations. You now can use this new-found habit to get your foot in the door with professors and professionals alike. We just have to tweak it a little first.

Instead conversing with faculty or a professional

over some trivial matter, try to keep the simple conversations you have on the topic of what they do in their research or career. By asking them good, pertinent, and intelligent questions throughout the conversation, you express your interest in that line of work, and thus build professional rapport. Quickly you will find that you can add to the conversation your own interest in that same field! If you can add to the conversation your own perspective, you generate a sort of "work experience" that they will bookmark in their mind. You don't even need to tell them that you are looking for a job just yet. Focus on building the relationship first. Show your hand only at the end of the card game, not at the beginning. If you do this regularly and consistently, preferably with the same people, you will be at the forefront of their mind when it comes to hiring or finding undergrad research assistants or prospective employees. Not to mention, if you ask them for their help in one of your own endeavors they will be more than likely to lend a hand. That's how you beat the networking Catch-22.

Conclusion

We covered in this chapter a bare-bones way to make networking a natural part of your life. To build rapport and thus eventual working relationships with professors, professionals, or just people in general, all it takes is *repeated, brief, conversational interactions.* Perhaps it will also take a little stepping out of your comfort zone as well. But, for example, if you can make use of your professor's office hours or the five minutes after class just to chat briefly every now and then, you will have your foot in the door when it comes to building a *working* relationship with them. In turn, you secure all sorts of solid recommendations.

Section D: Student Hacks

Chapter 17: Course Scheduling Hacks

Here in this chapter, we will discuss a few course scheduling strategies. We will also be taking a look at several different types of psychologies that are involved when a student picks their classes and how we can come up with a class schedule that takes advantage of them.

Strategy 1: Spread Out Your (easy) Gen-Eds

This is a pretty general rule of thumb and is applicable to nearly every student. Most undergrad programs require you to take a rather large number of gen-eds that range through humanities, sciences, mathematics, arts, religion, etc. And because there are often so many of these, you can take one or two a semester, every semester until you graduate. And the reason I'm telling you to spread them out is because in most cases **they are easy courses**, that is, if you do your research and pick them right. There are of course exceptions to this. Your science and math gen-eds will typically be harder and more work intensive, so be careful about those! But in general, for non-science/math intro courses, it is easier to succeed. They typically don't expect the same level of work as someone who is majoring in those topics. There are always exceptions, so do your research and talk to your peers. If you spread out your easy classes, you won't end up with a higher concentration of harder classes in any given semester. This can ease the burden of your college experience significantly.

Strategy 2: Don't Schedule 8am's

This is especially true for those who tend to stay up later (aka: all college students). If you are a student who frequently stays up late working on assignments or having fun, knowing you have to be awake by 7:55am (giving you just enough time to teleport to class) is a buzz kill. Moreover, as the semester drags on, if you find your willpower slipping and fatigue increasing, the first class you are going to skip is that 8am. I know this happened to me! I ended up skipping half a semester of chemistry one year (still passed the class thankfully). So to prevent such from happening, nip it in the bud and don't schedule too early classes if you can help it.

Strategy 3: Spread Your Courses Widely Across the Day

This is especially useful if you are prone to not studying after you have finished all your classes for the day. For example, you may want to schedule your earliest class at 10am and your last class to end at 5pm. That way, you can study in between your classes and get more schoolwork done as well.

You may be very tempted to go back to your dorm/home, somewhere crowded or somewhere with Facebook between your classes. So to help assuage this, simply commit to staying on campus in a work-conducive environment between classes. You don't even have to commit to working during that time. Just commit to being in a good work environment. Just being in that environment will encourage you to study and do quality work. Like all little habits, starting small, such as making a habit to be in a work environment even if you aren't using it to work necessarily, will build momentum and make growing that habit into something more productive far less cumbersome.

Strategy 4: Take Challenging Classes Earlier in the Day

This tip may seem contrary to common sense. As it turns out according to research, people think most effectively around the 10am mark, assuming they wake around 7-8am. So as long as you are relatively consistent in your sleep schedule (See: Sleep), plan to take your harder classes around 2 to 3 hours after you usually rise-and-shine. This hack takes full advantage of your body-clock (aka Circadian Rhythms) and will in turn yield you more success in classes that are typically more difficult.

Strategy 5: DON'T Schedule Hard Classes in the Mid-Afternoon

This hack mirrors the last, psychologically. The same research mentioned above cites that your brain is the most fatigued in the mid-to-late afternoon. This in turn leaves you less able to focus and learn as effectively as other times in the day. Not to mention you probably just had lunch, which in a boring or hard class will leave you catatonic at times. Leave the mid-afternoon for Intro to Painting or something that isn't as taxing mentally.

In general, the rule of thumb in this and the last strategy can be generalized a bit. You will be most productive if you do your bigger, more effort/brain-intensive tasks first thing in the day. Your willpower is a finite resource. As the day drags on, decisions and work become harder and harder. Thus, focus your harder tasks in the morning and your easier ones in the afternoon/evening. This will likely leave you feeling less drained by the end of the day.

Strategy 6: Research Your Professors

The best tool I know of for researching your professors is www.ratemyprofessor.com. This site is a collaborative forum of sorts where students will rate their professors on a basis of easiness, clarity, and helpfulness, and lets students fill in a short description of their experience with the professor in question. Using this tool will allow you to gauge the quality of education you will receive from that professor, and will help you to determine how easy or hard the class will be. And once you are done with a class, definitely make time to add feedback to this site! Most professors like to hear feedback, and some will read this site to get a "real feel" for what their students actually think of their teaching. Oh, and it's completely anonymous.

Chapter 18: Using Your Brain to the Fullest

Your brain in many ways is like a muscle. With repetition and effort exerted, it will grow and adapt to new stresses placed upon it. This includes willpower, rapid calculations; episodic, working, short-term, and long-term memory; relationship forming, stress responses, any conditionable behavior, and vastly many more. You can strengthen nearly every part of your brain simply by using it enough. And if you apply memorization strategies that, by themselves, enhance your ability to retain information, your brain will get even better at using those strategies. This will result in enhanced cognition that to you seemed impossible not too long ago.

In this chapter, we will be discussing ways that you

can improve your ability to memorize information efficiently and permanently. The techniques that follow consist of tactics and habits that, if used consistently and eventually mastered, will result in a far superior ability to learn and retain information. You will look back after not too long and realize that your brain is capable of far more now than it ever was before. This is not a sales pitch, but a promise to those who consistently apply what is covered.

Impact of Exercise, Sleep and Stress

It should be first mentioned that, in order to successfully maximize the power of your brain, other aspects such as sleep, exercise, and stress play a huge role in how effectively your brain works.

If you have ever been badly sleep deprived, you know that focusing or learning is next to impossible. Unfortunately, research shows that even if you are only mildly sleep deprived that your memory and cognitive abilities decline. It's even worse if you are *chronically* sleep deprived (that is, sleep deprived for over weeks to months). While you may be able to strengthen your cognitive abilities in this state, a simple change in your sleep habits could make all the difference. (See: Sleep)

The exact same situation as with sleep applies to stress as well. If you are stressed, even briefly, the hormones in your brain prevent it from functioning optimally. Think of the last time you had to take a test that was worth a hefty portion of your grade. Odds are you weren't exactly comfortable while taking it. You probably also noticed that half the information that you thought you knew suddenly vanished. Blame your body's stress response system for that one. If you are in a stressful situation, your brain is trying to get you out of that situation rather than to help you endure it. In turn, your memory declines. And also similar to sleep, if you are chronically anxious or stressed (or just drink too much coffee on average), your brain is always going to under-perform when you need it to work at its best. Your brain will do its finest work when you are the most at-ease.

Research has also shown that exercise plays a key role in the functionality of your brain. Students who exercise more on average tend to increase their memory and their abilities to perform cognitively. Hitting the gym a few times per week will reap you the cognitive advantage built into your very DNA.

Chunking

This is perhaps the most commonly cited method for improving short-term memory. It works basically as its name prescribes. You break a piece of information down into meaningful "chunks" that renders the bigger piece easier to memorize. For example, suppose you have a series of numbers such as 1812149234 that you want to quickly memorize. Instead of breaking it down into individual digits, you break it into more manageable pieces, such as 1812-1492-34 because the first make you think of the War of 1812, and the second relates to "when Columbus sailed the oceans blue." The last piece you relate to the age of your favorite actor. That's merely one example. As it turns out, just the act of breaking a larger piece of information into more manageable bits helps with memorizing *even if the pieces don't relate to anything.* That is, in the case above, simply breaking the string of digits down into parts of length 4 or fewer renders the whole string easier to remember even if you couldn't relate the numbers to anything. This idea is widely applicable. For another example, if you have vocab terms to memorize, focus on clusters of 3 or 4 words at a time, then move to the next cluster. If you hone this ability and can do it quickly, phone numbers and addresses and other strings of information will be easy to remember.

Relating

This is similar to the above, but is sufficiently more general. As mentioned before in "How to use class time effectively" in section B, one of the best ways you can learn new information quickly is to relate it to something you already understand. Like for example, in Biology, you learn about the different types of cells in both animals and plants. If you want to remember which cell type has a "cell wall" you could *relate* "cell wall" to "tree bark" in order to remember that *plant cells* have a cell wall. Never again will you forget this little tidbit of information. The thought pattern for this strategy is "what is this concept *similar to.*" It doesn't matter if the relationship is obvious or even a realistic relationship! If you can somehow relate cumulus cloud systems to a BMW, then it counts!

The information in your brain works like a braided rope (Hey! An example!). When you try to learn something new, your brain tries to find a way to connect that new idea to information already in your brain. So for each thing you relate to that new piece of information, you are adding another strand to the braid. And as braids work, the more strands you have, the stronger the braid; ergo, the stronger the new information sticks inside your head.

Relating Information to Yourself/Your Life

While the above tip has it so you are relating new information to stuff you already know, this tip has you relating new information to yourself and your own life; things you know so well and so personally that it goes beyond mere concept. Because the experiences you have in life are ridden with emotion, thought and vivid imagery, to associate something you are trying to learn to a particular memory can tie *all of that information* to it. And not too surprisingly, emotion is one of the strongest mechanisms by which information can be learned.

To exemplify the power of emotional learning, note that when someone is attacked with a knife, they can't really remember the face of their aggressor, as research shows. But they *can* remember, however, the weapon with astonishing accuracy even though they had seen the knife only fleetingly. Another example can be made of when you first fell in love. When a person falls in love, they are able to remember a vast majority of what their love interest has to say when compared to a neutral speaker. So by tying new information to emotional memories, such as a fantastic experience that you had while spending time with friends, you are deeply engaging this new information and rendering it far easier to recollect later.

Move!

This tip engages the motor control part of your brain and wires the information you need to know directly into your peripheral nervous system. For many people, and especially those who are tactile learners (those who learn by touching/doing things), it is often easier to remember information if it is something you can do with your body in some way. For example, you may have learned your "6,7,8, and 9's tables" for multiplication by using your fingers in a certain way, or you can tell your left from right by holding up both hands and checking which hand makes an "L" shape with the thumb and forefinger. While you may not know your left from right without having to check, you *do know* that your hands will give you the answer to that question. As it turns out, we can use this same strategy for many things we need to learn.

Suppose you need to learn the word "Chasseur" for French class. But this word is one of many on your list and it doesn't sound like anything you can think of in English. You read that it means "Hunter", so to help remember it, you quickly draw out and aim your imaginary rifle and say "Chasseur!" Then you do the same thing when you say "Hunter!" This wires the two words to that motion in your brain, and you are far less likely to forget it! This is just one example of how this technique can be used. If you can create bodily motion to associate with what you are learning, you will be able to remember it much more easily. This also may be why some people talk with their hands more than others! It may actually help them to find words in their mind as they speak.

One rule of thumb for using this technique is that you should exaggerate the motions you use. Like in the case of "Chasseur", drawing the imaginary rifle quickly emphasizes the readiness and vigilance of the hunter. There is more in the motion that the word can relate to than, say, if you were to limply raise your arms up into the sky. This is especially important if you have similar motions for different things.

Sing a Song

Seriously! For whatever reason, humans are incredibly adept at learning things via music and rhythm. Think of the last song you learned all the lyrics to. How long did it take you to remember it? I'd be willing to bet that you only had to hear that song maybe 4-5 times at most and read the lyrics once (maybe) in order to memorize a vast majority of the song. Suppose you instead you only read the lyrics. How long would that take you? So the next time you need to remember a complicated formula, such as, say, the Quadratic Formula in algebra, put it to a tune as you read it aloud (This formula works exceedingly well with "Pop Goes the Weasel")! You may have learned all the presidents of the United States or the entire Periodic Table of Elements via a song at some point. It may feel silly to sing to yourself about a rather long physics formula, but the tool of song is simply too powerful to waste.

If singing a song feels too silly for you, you can still take advantage of what is hard-wired into the human psyche via music, and more specifically, rhythm. If you are trying to remember a long formula, say it aloud to yourself with a beat. That is, tap on the desk at a consistent pace as you say the formula aloud. Perhaps you can nod your head instead so as to not distract anyone around you. Whether you decide to use rhythm or song (even if you have to invent a tune), either is an indispensable tool when it comes to memorizing.

Listen to Music

Perhaps in the past you have studied for an exam while listening to a particular artist or style of music. Perhaps then, strangely enough, you heard the same music in your head while you were actually taking the exam. It's an odd but not too surprising subconscious phenomenon. While you are studying while listening to music, you are subconsciously associating the information you are reviewing to the music playing in the background. This happens automatically and is almost entirely out of your control. But thankfully we can use this to trigger the *reverse!* That is, since taking an exam can bring a tune to mind, we can think of the tune first and it will bring needed information to mind. More accurately, it may not bring *exact facts* to mind (though it can), but it will make it easier to recall material overall.

To get the best results, study with music playing

quietly in the background (preferably headphones) so as to not distract you. Pick one artist of style of music for each subject you are studying. This makes it easier to recall more specific and pertinent information. That way, you won't be thinking about Intro to Agronomy while sitting in an Algebra test. For *even better* results, play one song on repeat for each distinct topic you are learning for that class. Then when you get to your exam or when you want to try to recall that information, you can essentially go through a "playlist" of very specific material in your mind by simply remembering a song.

In summary, we have discussed a variety of different memory hacks that can aid you virtually instantly the moment you apply them. But as mentioned before, each of the above is a skill that can be grown with continued usage. That is, you can actually get even more out of your brain if you practice the above tips on a regular basis. Moreover, with consistent practice, your brain will start doing these automatically and you won't even have to think about it. I've seen people who have mastered just one or two of the tactics mentioned above, and they are able to learn in ways I can't even comprehend. They humbly state that they are just using one or two methods, and that the only difference between them and most people is that they can do it insanely fast. Speed necessarily comes with practice.

Chapter 19: Procrastination

Procrastination. We all do it to some degree or another. We all have had that assignment or exam that is on the horizon but we simply cannot muster up the willpower needed to start working. We know we need to get started earlier rather than later, but for some reason things end up getting done the day before it is due. We find clever little ways, either subconsciously or consciously, to put things off until the last minute. This happens even though we know getting started on the night before is going to be a living hell that results in sleep deprivation, likely a poorly done assignment, or half-assed study. We procrastinate for a wide variety of reasons, surely not limited to:

1) Distractions that are more appealing than the work you need to do (i.e. Facebook).

2) A need to do things perfectly, which halts starting

altogether

3) The task that needs done is tedious and/or seemingly unimportant

4) The task is unpleasant overall and it feels best to do that which is most comfortable

5) A belief that you are inadequate or will do an inadequate job

6) A lack of motivation or interest overall

7) A fear of what may result of doing really well (fear of success is a real thing)

8) A fear of failure

9) Feeling overwhelmed

10) Feeling a need to work on other easier tasks unrelated to that which you are putting off

Likely, one of the above will resonate with you at some point or another when it comes to needing to get something done. Thankfully, there is a vast array of tactics that you can employ to overcome nearly any one of the above reasons for procrastination. This chapter will detail a few tried-and-true methods for overcoming the itch to put things off.

Promise Yourself 5-10 Minutes of Work

This is a clever way of tricking your brain into getting started. Tell yourself that you are going to put in 5 to 10 minutes (or some very short time period < 20 minutes) and then you can choose to continue to work or stop working. You are giving yourself permission to not work after that time period. More accurately, you are giving yourself the option to reevaluate once that time period is up. But commit yourself to that small amount of time. More likely than not, you will find yourself wanting to keep going after those 5-10 minutes, so keep up the good work! But make sure that you commit to those few minutes and get started immediately! Don't push those few minutes of work into the future. That would defeat the purpose.

Deliberately Plan When You Are Going to Work

This can work in conjunction with the aforementioned tip. Either at the start of your day or the night before, schedule the part of your day where you are going to work on school related assignments or study. Determine the exact hour and make it a part of your schedule for the day (See: Scheduling). Then once that hour rolls around, use the tip above to get yourself going. You will be amazed how quickly you build momentum. You will also be proud of yourself for so readily getting to work!

Eliminate Distractions

This one is fairly obvious. Get yourself far away from a computer, or at least close all windows relating to

Facebook or YouTube. Turn off your phone. Yes, completely turn it off. You don't need it while you are studying or working. Put yourself in a location that is quiet that lends itself well to focusing; a place that is free of distraction.

The above may feel rather harsh. I personally don't want to force myself into a situation where I don't have a computer. I like the idea that I can hop on Facebook the moment I hit a wall in my work or study. If you are like me in this way, there is a middle ground between having the ability to procrastinate on your computer or phone and being in a perfectly distraction-free setting. See the following tip!

Set an End Time within Study/Work Sessions

One of the biggest reasons I procrastinated in college is because I never gave myself a time where I can call it quits. Ergo, I was working constantly and ceaselessly. I knew if I started working that I wouldn't feel like I was allowed to take breaks. I would feel guilty. Who on earth wants to have their nose to the grindstone from dawn to dusk? The solution to this I've found is simply to set a time at which you will allow yourself to relax and take a break. This is guilt-free time wasting! The human mind is only capable of focusing intently for 20-40 minutes at any given time. We burn out remarkably quickly. So for every 40 minutes you decide to work, commit to stopping for a little bit to recharge. You can use your recharge time for anything you like. It is important to eventually get started again of course. Refer to the first tip every time you want to get started on your work.

Break Tasks and Assignments Down

At times you will have an assignment or a huge exam that is just so huge that you can't even begin to imagine how you are going to get it done by the deadline or how you are going to study so much material in such a short time. Instead of focusing on the big picture, see if you can break the huge amount of work you have to do into smaller pieces. Break things down into a series of steps that are much more reasonable in size and tractability. If even those steps seem too huge, break them down even smaller! Write all these steps down on paper. Whatever you do, do not focus on the number of steps or the whole project! Focus only on the first task that you need to get done and get started on it as soon as possible. Focusing only on the smaller pieces will keep you moving through the project or study material with incredible momentum. You will feel a sense of achievement for each step you complete, and you will feel motivated to complete the next step!

Get an Accountability Buddy

There is a saying: "Success comes in pairs of two." So if you find yourself a study buddy, you can hold each other accountable and keep one another honest. You don't need to even be working on the same class or topic to do this, just find a friend that you wouldn't mind working alongside (preferably one who won't distract you). Schedule times together that you both will commit to working during the day and meet up at that time. It is much harder to break study plans with someone else than it is with yourself. If you think of breaking your plans, just think of your friend sitting alone wherever you agreed to study, thinking to themselves that it would have been really helpful to have someone to work beside. They need you as much as you need them. It is so incredibly useful to have people holding each other accountable. You will be amazed at how much more work you can get done when you work with someone else.

Set Deadlines before the Real Deadline

By setting a deadline earlier and sticking to it, you guarantee that you will both get the task done on time, and will be more prompt about starting it. This will work even if you put things off until the last minute! If you set your deadline (literally do this in your calendar) two days early, even if you wait until the night before, you still will have it done two days in advance. At which point, you can take those extra days to improve upon your work.

Focus on the End-Game Success

If you ever feel unmotivated to start an assignment or to start studying, take a few moments to daydream. Think about all that will result from you finishing your assignment or your studies. Imagine in vivid detail the feeling of destroying your exam and the relief you will feel once it is all over. Think about that awesome feeling of successfully completing your assignment well before it is due, knowing you won't have to ever think about it again. What will finishing your task bring you? Will you be better in that subject? Will your grade improve as a result of a job well done? Will you have more time to yourself once you finish? Have you set up a reward for yourself if you finish? Will it be one more victory in your battle versus chronic procrastination? Keep all these positive feelings, results, and images in your mind as you work and revisit them if you ever feel challenged to get started.

Conclusion

This list of tips is by no means comprehensive but it does contain the most effective methods for beating procrastination that I and my students use any time we find ourselves at a sticking point. Try a few. Change them to suit how your mind works. If you can consistently beat procrastination in our world so full of distraction, you are far and away more advanced on your way to success than most people in society.

Chapter 20: Sleep Your Way to Success

Ahhh yes! The #1 thing that nearly everyone neglects. Because we can seemingly function on little, and can often accomplish tasks when entirely sleep deprived, we treat this essential part of our biology as negligible and tedious. College students are by no means exempt. We all know and have been told time and time again that sleep is important and it helps with everything and yada, yada, yada but we really don't want to hear it, do we? We think that we can do just as well sleeping when we have no other choice and having fun or being productive is more compelling. But as we will discuss below, it turns out that you can use sleep to your advantage and that if you are consistent with your sleep habits, you in fact can do much more with your day than if you pulled all-nighters or slept less on average per night.

Because nearly every college student is already in a sleep deprived state, we are instead of warning against the issues that could result from a lack of sleep, we will instead discuss the benefits of consistent (falling asleep and awaking at the same time every day) 8 hours/night sleep because, after all, we are more often interested in what we can gain than what we can forgo.

Benefits of Consistent Sleep

-Better Memory (who doesn't want that???)

-Increased work efficiency

-Mood stability

-Increased focus and clarity of mind.

-increased willpower, drive, motivation

-Increased creativity

-Less risk for depression

-Reduced blood pressure

-Reduced anxiety

-Reduced cortisol production (stress hormone which correlates with weight gain)

-Easier body weight control

-Increased Human Growth Hormone production (good for those who want to put on muscle)

-Increased lifespan

-Aids warding off cancer (those who sleep less are at greater risk)

-Just a generally better life.

A wide array of benefits right? All these can be yours for just 8 hours a day.

Consistent and Sufficient Sleep: An Invitation

It should be briefly mentioned that while many experts claim we need 8 hours of sleep per night, they often fail to mention the huge impact of CONSISTENT sleep and wake times. Current research shows that consistency is actually more important than the number of hours you sleep per night! That is, even if you get 8 hours of sleep every day, but at weird times, you will likely feel as groggy as if you had only gotten a handful of hours. This has the same effect of subjecting yourself to jet lag on a constant basis.

Now you may be thinking "but I get anywhere from 6 to 8 hours a night with varying bedtime and I feel great and I get by just fine!" You only THINK you do! Odds are you have lacked a sleep schedule for so long that you forgot what normal feels like! Whether you want to admit it or not, those who have no set sleep schedule nor get enough sleep are operating at only a fraction of their true potential. And seeing that you are in school, you want to make the most of every ounce of brain you have between your ears. Thus, based on everything I just mentioned, I strongly encourage and implore you to get on a regular sleep schedule and stick to it. I will personally guarantee you it will pay dividends in the long run and will likely help you improve your grades and study habits as well. The benefits you will reap are plenty and all it takes is some self-discipline.

But how do we get on a schedule when life is so busy and school work is as unpredictable as it comes? Here's a very rudimentary guide to setting up and initializing a consistent sleep schedule:

1) Committing to a Wake Time

Everyone is different in terms of what will work for them biologically and what works with their schedule/workload. You may have three days out of five a week where you have an 8am class, but the earliest class you have on the other two days may be in the afternoon. The temptation is to get up early to go to your 8am when you had stayed up late the night before, then "make it up" the other two to four days. Or worse, over time you will start skipping your 8am class as the semester gets harder (and it will). This is so bad!! While you may be able to average 8 hours of sleep throughout the week, your body will never be able to recover its standard biological clock timing and you will live in a constant state of jet lag. If your earliest class is 8am for just ONE DAY of the entire week, guess what? You need to wake up at the same time *every single day*, as if you were going to that 8am class (pick your classes wisely). This includes weekends too! If you can't make this happen once or twice a month, that is okay! Life and parties happen. Your body will adapt to one rare day of skimped sleep at a time. Two, and you will regret it I assure you.

The reason that committing to a wake time is first on this list is because the first day or two, you may already be going to bed at 4am on a semi-regular basis. The first couple days you will be in sleep deficit if you commit to an early rise time (such as 8am, early for most college students) and that's good! You WILL be fatigued throughout the first day. But by the time you get to sleep in the evening, you will be able to crash immediately rather than needing to count sheep. Resist the urge to nap, and prevent it at all costs. All you need to do is fight it for one day. You can do that for certain.

2) Committing to a To-Bed Time That Also Fits Your Schedule and Assures At Minimum 7 Hours of Sleep

As with finding a solid waking time, find a non-negotiable to-bed time that matches your wake time so that you score at least 7 hours, ideally 8. You may be thinking "but my course load won't let me do that! I have to do homework and study every night into the wee hours of the morning in order to keep up!" My personal excuse for not getting on a schedule was for the longest time "If I go to bed early and try to finish my work the next day, there is no guarantee that I will be able to finish it in time!" You may sympathize with one of these or something similar. If that is the case, simply adjusting your sleep schedule may indeed cause problems with your coursework. Something else, in turn, will need to change as well. See section "Having enough time in a day." Just keep in mind throughout the next couple weeks all the benefits of consistent and sufficient sleep, and know that habits get easier, both bodily and mentally, over time.

Warning! The first week or two of readjusting to this normal sleep schedule will be really challenging and you may find yourself even more fatigued at times, but if you commit to it for two weeks, you will have fully reset your body clock. If you aren't feeling more alive and alert after that time frame, you can decide what you want to do from there. Just commit to two weeks and then at the end you can re-evaluate.

3) Following a Pre-Bedtime Routine

This is an advanced tactic and a good idea. It by no means needs to be established with the above two steps (See: Habits). Come up with a list (in order of activity) of things you absolutely must have done before bed to set yourself up for success the following morning and can put you at ease before attempting shuteye. The following example is my personal pre-bed routine:

1) Wipe kitchen counters and put all dishes away

2) Tidy apartment and clear work areas or clutter

3) Feed cat

4) Shower and brush teeth

5) Fill water bottle

6) Set up coffee for morning

7) Lay out clothes for next day

8) Read in bed for 15 minutes

9) Pray

10) Meditate my way to sleep

This routine takes me roughly 30-40 minutes to complete depending on how messy my kitchen is. By no means does your list have to take as long, but for this to be effective. For the first few weeks of doing this, make sure you do not put other tasks into the routine spontaneously. It's best to make a habit of it so it becomes muscle memory to get to bed. Just find something that gets you to relax and stick with it. Here are a few more ideas that you may like to include in your list:

- Plan your tasks for the next day, and review first thing in the morning
- Drink (caffeine free) tea

- Yoga (the slow, no sweat version)

- Turn off all machines and screens (usually a good idea 30 minutes to an hour before bed)

- Review the successes of the day you just completed

- Pack lunch for the next day

- Deep breathing exercises

Just remember to keep this list simple and relaxing. Stick with the above three steps for exactly two weeks and do not falter if you can help it. If at the end you want to not run your sleep schedule this way, simply reevaluate and change things up. You know your body and your life better than anyone, so you gotta do what works for you.

Tips for Getting Better, Quality Sleep

Below follows a list of sleep-hacks pooled from a variety of sources designed to improve the quality of your sleep and to shorten the amount of time it takes to actually nod off. As with any habit or behavior you want to change, take them only one or two at a time and maintain consistency if you want to see lasting change.

1) Cut the lights 30 minutes to an hour before bed.

Reduce the amount of light in your living space and all sources of harsh light. Since your goal is to eventually sleep, your brain needs to produce enough melatonin to start the process and keep you asleep. How do you increase melatonin production? Cut the light. The pineal gland in the brain is responsible for melatonin production and is light sensitive. It has cones and rods much in the same way your eyes do, but it doesn't handle light directly of course. It handles the signal of light coming from your eyes and produces or inhibits melatonin production to follow suit with the environment. Hence the next tip also applies using this same mechanism.

2) Sleep when it's dark out or invest in thick drapes

As before, we are trying to limit the amount of light in your environment close to when you want to be snoozing. So by taking advantage of the natural cycles built into your biology, you will get better sleep. Moreover, sleeping at night is better than dense drapery because the light first thing in the morning will also reach your eyes, signaling the wake-up procedure in your brain. We were built to be diurnal, and working against that framework does more harm than good in most cases.

3) No caffeine 3-4 hours prior to bedtime

I don't care if you can handle enough caffeine on a regular basis to kill a large bear or that you experience little effect from it, caffeine effects your sleep quality if it's in your system when you hit the pillow. Myself and others have found that it is best to avoid stimulants 3-4 hours prior to bedtime due to this. If you are feeling tired before bed, GOOD! You're supposed to. If you simply must be productive in the evening and need the extra kick, drink low caffeine tea. Just avoid high concentrations of caffeine if you want to see a change.

4) Don't exercise before bed

I am very guilty of this. With a gym attached to my apartment complex and 24 hours/day access, and the knowledge that my body will feel quite tired after a quick bout of picking heavy things up and putting them down, it seemed like a good idea. Unfortunately, exercise excites brain activity even if your body is fatigued. Physical actually sharpens your focus and overall energy levels which is exactly what you DON'T want while heading to bed. It will be more than challenging to get to sleep quickly.

5) Avoid meals or even snacks 4 hours before bed

Ever hear someone tell you to never eat cheese or dairy before bed because it will cause bad dreams and tossing and turning? Well there is a good deal of truth to that. In general when you eat in the hours before bed, your metabolism spikes in activity level in order to digest food. This goes for all foods and especially ones hard to digest like cheeses and dairy. People tend to think that digestion is a gastrointestinal process and that is quarantined to that system in the body. It's not. Different hormones spike and fall, blood flow changes throughout the body, the immune system reacts differently, and many different systems of neurons in your body are all teeming just to digest that macaroni and cheese you just had to have before bed because you were starving. Additionally, you have a series of chemicals that are being released into your bloodstream from the food you just ate. Because digestion is a whole-body process and your body has to perform to break down food into simple nutrients it certainly is going to affect your sleep patterns in a wide variety of ways. This of course differs from food to food, but the general rule of thumb suggested here is to not eat anything in the hours before bed.

Additionally, there is some research that states that not eating before bed can help with weight loss as your body will use fat as energy while you sleep and won't be storing the last meal you ate as you lie there for 8 hours. While there is research supporting this notion, like most things in the fitness industry, the jury is still out on the true effectiveness of this strategy and any 'proof' is likely to change in the coming months anyway. Though, I can say from my own experience that this method has worked. So why not give a risk-free strategy a try?

6) To fall asleep quickly, try this deep breathing exercise.

This strategy is incredible. I prided myself in being a lifelong insomniac, not by choice but simply because I couldn't get my brain to stop running full tilt while I stared at my ceiling. I came upon this strategy one day and I've been able to fall asleep consistently within ten minutes of lying down. The "6-7-8" strategy is as follows:

1) Get comfortable, in a position you sleep well in.
2) inhale for 6 seconds through your nose enough to fill your lungs but not painfully so
3) Hold your breath for 7 seconds
4) release your breath over 8 seconds
5) rinse and repeat

When I do this, I am usually asleep before the 10th set. It just works like magic. This breathing technique purportedly lowers your heart rate significantly, and while slowing and deepening your breathing, it puts your body in a state very similar to sleep before your brain eventually catches up.

As with most things written in this book, the above are a set of simple strategies that can vary from person to person, and will almost certainly depend on your particular situation. So feel free to change things up a bit and find some awesome plan of attack that works for you!

Using Sleep to your Academic Advantage

Here we will discuss how we can use the power of sleep paired with the mysterious workings of the subconscious mind to enhance learning, retention, problem solving, and ultimately help you get better grades.

The Power of (short) Naps

While I said in the last section to avoid naps, this is one exception: when the naps span no more than 30 minutes at a time. These will not impact your sleep at night terribly. These naps are not meant to boost energy levels as much (though they can), and if you are already sleep deprived they can make you feel more tired. But if you are on a solid sleep regime already or even if you are not and can tolerate mild fatigue well then you can benefit a bit from what's to come.

While Studying

If you find yourself studying for hours at a time, simply memorizing, or learning you can use a short (<30 minute) nap to help with the process! Your brain uses sleep for storing and arranging long-term memory, and since what you have been doing for the last several hours has been on the forefront of your mind and something you have been processing at length, your brain will use the short nap as time to store some of that! It will help lock your studies into your mind more effectively than if you simply bombarded your mind with more material for the next few hours. Think of it like a cup of coffee. You gotta drink what's in your cup before you try to fill it with more! Otherwise the coffee will spill out everywhere leaving you with less life-elixir overall.

The rule for this to be truly effective, however, is that your study must be consistent prior to your short nap. If you are half-assing your studies and browsing the Internet or doing something other than studying, your brain isn't focused on the material you are to be absorbing and thus A) will not store it while you are awake, and B) will not be able to manage the information you want it to while you nap (because there is little properly encoded into your short term memory in the first place). So remain truly focused for at least an hour or so prior to napping.

I've found personally that you can repeat this a few times if you are studying for long hours without it being detrimental to your sleep at night. I try to limit it to fewer than 4 naps per day. Otherwise, I definitely see a reduction in my sleep quality at night. This is entirely up to your biology and sleep habits of course, so find a system that works for you.

While Drilling Problems or Problem-Solving in General

I'm sure you've heard of people who had taken rest while working on a problem they were stuck on and then upon waking they suddenly had the answer. This isn't as much a stroke of genius but just the same biology mentioned above at play, and you can take advantage of it to have periodic “eureka” moments that would send you streaking through the streets more boldly than Archimedes himself.

Because when you are napping, your brain is processing short-term memory and storing it in long term memory, rearranging the neural pathways and making those paths as efficient as possible. And as part of this process, it may rearrange the information about the problem you are working on in such a way that the next time you think about your problem, new ways of thinking readily appear. Not necessarily will you have a solution instantly in hand, but you may have new perspective by which you can attack the problem. Countless times have I found myself struggling with the same problem for days (yes, hard homework problems in math can take hours to days to work out), and upon waking from a short nap I actually found myself significantly closer to a solution. Sometimes I had the solution in hand as well!

The most effective way I have personally found to make use of this faculty of the human mind is thus: get comfortable enough to fall asleep, but continue thinking about the problem as you nod off. It doesn't and shouldn't be intense thought, but just enough to keep the problem and related information in mind. I've found that your thoughts as you fall asleep while thinking about the problem become more and more loosely associated. Your mind is suddenly free to think creatively about the problem rather than trying to solve it outright.

Sleeping on your Studies

No not literally. We cannot learn by osmosis or by download just yet, though I am sure someone is working on that. But what we can do naturally is pretty close.

Say you have an exam coming up in the next week

and you need to retain as much information as humanly possible. Instead of cramming the night before (See: "How to Destroy Any Exam"), the week or two before the exam, spend a significant amount of time studying before bed. Good, honest, focused study; completely undistracted. If you have your evening routine down to muscle memory, by the time you lay down to sleep your brain will be teeming with new information that it is dying to process and store for the long haul much in the same way we discussed in the last section. Your brain will then have all 8 hours to process that information and fully encode it in your long term memory. And since your work has been at the pinnacle of your focus for the last several hours, your brain will process that information first and foremost. If you dream about studying, I deeply apologize.

Chapter 21: Conclusions

College is by no means an endeavor that one can take lightly. It offers many unique challenges, many of which you have never encountered yet in your entire life. These challenges are there for a reason and they are always disguising an opportunity. Every opportunity in life is masked by temporary discomfort, but it is still an opportunity nonetheless. The challenges you will face and likely have faced up until this point are there to build you up despite what it may seem like on the surface. You will become stronger and more resilient when you face new challenges as the years after college become the present.

Via your education you have been given a huge opportunity to grow yourself in so many awesome ways, but it is entirely up to you to make the most of it. It is so easy to coast through college and just pass your classes, put in the minimum effort and come out relatively unscathed with a degree in hand. This may be fine for so many college students but it should send off a red flag in your head. Why? Because you are here for a reason and you are here to see it through. You are here to put in more effort than anyone else because that's what it take to achieve what no one else can.

By using the tips outlined in this book, you will have cultivated a success-based mindset whereby you find the resources you need even when it seems like there is no help to be found; a mindset of staying uncomfortable for the sake of growth and making your dreams a reality; a mindset that leads you to be the hardest and most effective worker in any room. This mindset will take you further than you can imagine. It does not only apply to academia, but it will generalize and transfer to all domains of life such as marriage, finances, time management, on the job, etc. It is this mindset that has led thousands to achieve the life they dreamt of.

Now will you be the one in a thousand who walks instead of talks? Are you going to make the most of your education? Are you going to put in the effort and do whatever it takes to reach your goals in life thereafter? You are an amazing person with so many talents and gifts. You are destined for greatness; you really are. But it is entirely up to you to make your potential your reality. So I dare you to take a step forward into your dreams. I dare you to put in the effort and do what it takes without counting the cost. Why? Because I can promise you that it is worth it.

51828777R00172

Made in the USA
Middletown, DE
16 November 2017